INSTITUTE FOR WORKERS' CONTROL

PAMPHLETS 1-10 (1968)

Compiled by Jake Black and Tom Unterrainer

Michael Barratt Brown, Ken Coates, Lawrence Daly,
Bob Harrison, Walter Kendall, Ernest Mandel,
Hugh Scanlon, Tony Topham

Facsimile Edition

SPOKESMAN

This facsimilie edition of IWC pamphlets from 1968 is re-published in 2023 for the benefit of the public record and to meet the enduring interest in, and support for, democracy in the workplace.

Published by Spokesman Books
5 Churchill Park, Nottingham NG4 2HF, England
www.spokesmanbooks.org
www.socialistrenewal.net (online texts)

ISBN 9780851249285

Contents

IWC Pamphlet 1
The Way Forward for Workers' Control
Hugh Scanlon ... 1

IWC Pamphlet 2
Productivity Bargaining and Workers' Control
Tony Topham ... 11

IWC Pamphlet 3*
Labour and Sterling
Michael Barratt Brown ... 23

IWC Pamphlet 4
Opening the Books
Michael Barratt Brown ... 47

IWC Pamphlet 5
The Labour Party's Plans for Industrial Democracy
Ken Coates and Tony Topham ... 61

IWC Pamphlet 6
Workers' Control and the Motor Industry
Bob Harrison and Walter Kendall ... 71

IWC Pamphlet 7
Steel Workers Next Step
A Group of Sheffield Steel Workers ... 85

IWC Pamphlet 8
Industrial Democracy and National Fuel Policy
Institute for Workers' Control & Lawrence Daly ... 93

IWC Pamphlet 10†
A Socialist Strategy for Western Europe
Ernest Mandel ... 109

* IWC Pamphlet 3 has been transcribed from the original
† No 'IWC Pamphlet 9' was published

The Way Forward For Workers' Control

Hugh Scanlon

Institute for Workers' Control

Pamphlet Series No. 1   One Shilling and Sixpence   (7½p)

The Heart of the Matter
Bertrand Russell

I welcome the growing importance of the workers' control movement because its demands go to the heart of what I have always understood socialism to mean. The Prime Minister and his friends have developed a quite new definition of socialism, which includes the penalising of the poorest, capitulating to bankers, attacking the social services, banning the coloured and applauding naked imperialism. When a government makes opportunism the hallmark of its every action, it is the duty of all socialists to cry 'halt' and to help create an alternative based on socialist principles. In this urgent task I wish you every success.

The Way Forward to Workers' Control
Hugh Scanlon

The whole question of workers' control is once again becoming an important issue in the British Labour Movement. In some ways, the situation today is analogous to that before the First World War. Expansion of Industry, coupled with inflation, in the years up to 1914, provided the basis for aggressive union action and the growth of ideas concerning workers' control, culminating in a historic pamphlet, the 'Miners Next Step'. It provided the impetus for the growth of the Shop Steward Movement, which arose during the war years itself.

The depression of the inter war years, with the resultant high unemployment, produced a largely defensive struggle by the labour movement, with the unions concentrating on the vital function of attempting to defend minimum national rates of pay. In these adverse conditions, the demands for workers' control over their environment and industrial destinies, died hard. The T.U.C. in the 1930's was formally converted to the Morrisonian concept of the running of nationalised industries, as exemplified in the London Passenger Transport Bill. This denied direct workers' representation, a view only arrived at after long and bitter debate. Modifications to Morrison's views had to be made in the 1930's due to the strength of the opposition from many trade unions which called for 'workers participation through their Trade Unions in the direction and management of nationalised industry at all levels.'

After the 2nd World War, the T.U.C. reverted to its earlier position by abandoning demands for direct representation except on consultative bodies, for nationalised industries. This was a position that the then Labour Government in office fully shared. It is significant that in these years, dissident voices were raised, including unions such as the Union of Post Office Workers and the N.U.R. who had full experience of the type of 'Joint Consultation' practised in the nationalised industries. The only unionists on the Board of nationalised industries, as laid down in policy agreed by the T.U.C., were those who had formally severed connection with their own union. Direct representation by workers in management was completely excluded. The A.E.U. then, as now, rejected this approach. The A.E.U. spokesman at the 1948 Labour Party Conference stated that — "We have always argued in the Socialist Party that brains are not a monopoly of any particular class. I certainly believe and am convinced that there are sufficient brains within the Trade Union and Socialist movement to warrant a greater proportion of seats on the governing bodies of nationalised industries". There was an increasing recognition that if it were merely a case of trade union appointment by government there was great doubt whether such a change would influence ordinary workers, since there was no more of a direct link with new nominees than with the present ones.

The debate was interrupted, for all effective purposes, by the return of a Tory Government in 1951. Current interest can now be said to have revived not only because of the return of a new Labour Government, but because of important changes in the Labour Movement which can be seen as a product of the boom period itself. The British Labour Movement has changed from the days of the thirties. Never has the labour movement in this country been stronger, more confident and more experienced largely as a result, not only of technological change, and the integration of white collar 'specialists' within the Labour Movement, but because of relatively full employment. Trade Union membership has doubled since the 1930's and the increased confidence of workers has reflected itself in the development of strong shop floor organisations, which have been able not only to bargain very effectively for increased earnings at a local level, but also question the 'prerogative of management'.

There already exists, particularly in fully unionised industrial concerns, a considerable degree of workers' control in individual factories if 'workers' control' is defined as effective control by organised workers over the arbitrary powers of management. This is indeed 'the seeds of the new society inside the old'. Shop Stewards prefer, and seem to get more out of, workshop bargaining than the type of 'consultation' favoured by management. 'Joint consultation' committees tend to be limited by the assumption that — 'management should only agree to share responsibility on controversial and common interest issues, like manning, it cannot do more than consult'.[1] But workshop representatives see things very differently. Shop Stewards 'tend to believe that any subject which affects their members is a fit and proper matter for negotiations and agreement; they also are inclined to think that conflicts of interest can just as easily arise over questions such as the introduction of new machines or output levels as they can over wages and hours'.[2]

This radical move away from the defensive mentality of the past is graphically shown in the facts concerning the causes of industrial disputes. It has been shown that between 1940 and 1960, the proportion of strikes, (excluding strikes in the mining industry) not directly concerned with wage increases but connected with disputes such as about working arrangements, rules and discipline have risen from about one-third to three-quarters of the total. In 1960, a T.U.C. survey showed that only 32% of strikes were directly about money; 29% were about dismissals alone.

In this brief survey it is clear that the changes in the Labour Movement since the thirties is making nonsense of the concept of a purely 'economic man', limited to actions in defence of his standard of living. Far wider issues are involved today.

Yet even the extension of the current type of 'workers control' can be seen as holding only a watching and limiting function on the 'rights' of management. Workers are demanding an *effective* voice in management policy. This aspiration is particularly concentrated in regard to the nationalised industries, where obviously the greatest scope is offered for the demand that management be obliged to obtain the consent of workers in all matters of industrial policy. Trade unions envisage a radical extension of the scope of collective union action, from a point beyond wages and salaries to human conditions of employment in its broadest aspects.

It is in this light that union proposals on the structure of a nationalised steel industry, for example, are being based. The National Craftsmen's Co-ordinating Committee for the Iron and Steel Industry has submitted detailed proposals. Thus, at the Combine or group level it is proposed that the appointment of a head for the Operating Board should be subject to ratification by a Group Workers' Council. These Workers Councils, according to the N.C.C.C. proposal should be elected on a half and half basis from

1. Cf. W. McCarthy, Evidence to the Royal Commission on Trade Unions.
2. Ibid.

the appropriate trade unions and from shop, mill or office committees, and they should have the power to receive reports on all policies and to ask for detailed costings of all departments. At plant level, both the chairman and management representatives should be ratified by departmental committees or by the Workers Council, while half the membership should be drawn from elected workers' representatives. At shop, mill and office level, the proposals are even more radical. Indeed they urge that democratically elected committees should subject to ratification the appointment of shop managers and foremen, the deployment of labour, promotion, the hiring and dismissing of workers, safety, welfare and disciplinary matters. They should also have special responsibilities for training and education, and other responsibilities delegated from the combine or group workers council.

The machinery suggested gives workers and unions both the powers of scrutiny and of veto, and so allows for the extension of workers influence on management beyond the limitations of defensive collective bargaining. Yet even on the most democratic system of workers' influence on management beyond the limitations of defensive such as the steel industry, serious problems must be faced. One problem is of course the perpetual dilemma of trade unions in discussing the question of workers' self management, in that trade unions cannot easily double the part of protective agencies, democratically responsible to their members and required to carry out their membership's wishes, on the one hand, and joint policy makers and managers of industry; responsible to the public at large for efficiency and increased production, on the other.

But perhaps the most immediate problem so far as workers' control in the nationalised industries is concerned, is the position of these industries in a predominantly private enterprise economy. The evidence is overwhelming that nationalised industries in the past have been used primarily for the benefit of private industry. There is the problem of the run-down of some of these industries, such as coal. In the case of steel, the Benson Committee estimated that while the industry produced 27 million tons of steel in 1965 with 317,000 workers, in 1975 the estimated figures are 35.3 million tons with 215,000 workers. This one example underlines a fundamental dilemma; what is to happen to workers in a declining industry and how would the problem be approached and solved under workers' control?

So one is forced to take a wider view than that of workers' control in the present nationalised industries. It is questionable whether such control can ever be effective within a specific sector without the 'commanding heights' of the economy coming into public ownership. Indeed without public ownership of the major sectors of industry, a rational basis for effective planning, which will allow a full system of workers' self-management and control, cannot be fully implemented. If the nationalised industries are dependent on the working of the whole economy, and if the economy is dominated, in its largest sectors, by private ownership, even the most democratic system of workers' control in an industry such as steel has built-in limitations.

So we are compelled to examine the prospects for workers' control in the major, private sectors, of the economy. Even in the most 'progressive' firms in the private sectors, 'workers participation' tends to run up against a brick-wall when it comes to the most vital aspects of company policy and managerial functions. Workers are held to have 'rights' to welfare, representation of grievances, and a share in those aspects of policy-making which do not challenge profit-making, while employers have 'rights' to dispose of their property, including the labour they hire, according to managerial policy. This conception gives rise to the 'separate spheres of interest' formulation which undermines all schemes for workers' participation and thus limits the scope of joint consultative bodies. There is still, in all essentials, the preservation of financial, technological and long term planning functions from any workers' veto.

Full consultation of this nature, though progressive, can only be a pale shadow of workers' full participation. Obviously trade unionists should support any method of consultation in private industry that limits the arbitary decision-making of management and extends social accountability. But recent developments have sharply outlined that the power of management to unilaterally take decisions completely contrary to workers' needs and aspirations is in reality unchanged. The recent spate of big mergers and their methods of 'rationalisation' place the most elementary needs of job-security in danger. The example of the A.E.I. closure at Woolwich shows the futility of a blind faith that these giant monopolies will acknowledge pressures for social accountability. Only full public ownership can give both workers and the general public control over these vast combines. Only through nationalisation of these giant monopolies can both effective planning on a national level, and an effective system of industrial democracy, to supplement the shell of political democracy (itself a product of the struggles of the working-class movement) be properly and effectively carried forward. The nationalisation of the basic industries under 'workers' control at all levels' is official A.E.F. policy. The Labour movement cannot rest contented with a tenuous and limited say merely in the functioning of welfare facilities. This is particularly true in the present industrial climate of larger and larger monopolies, only really accountable to their own shareholders, who may well become a threat to political democracy itself. In this connection the slogan of 'open the books' to allow accredited workers' representatives to pursue the financial ramifications of these vast combines is a concrete first step towards the development of social accountability.

One cannot give any kind of detailed blueprint for such a radical transformation as a transition to a socialist society under full democratic workers' self management; what we can do is to analyse certain tendencies and safeguards that can be the basis of proposals to map our route without falling into the twin traps of local free-for-alls and excessive centralisation. Certainly with nationalisation, workers must not be made to feel, as they certainly do at present, that there is only a political change while there remains an industrial status quo. Fundamentally, the aim within public ownership is the wearing down of sides in industry, with no 'superiors' or 'inferiors' but only differences and functions based on knowledge and ability. Only through public ownership could there be this real will to co-operate.

There need be no real contradiction between the necessity for integration and centralisation of resource planning in a modern developed economy, and a structure of democratic decision-making that allows flexibility and the development of local initiative. It seems a false assumption to counter-pose the two. Indeed the decentralised 'market' criteria of the Yugoslav pattern constrain the workers' freedom in work (irrespective of works-council decisions) and hamper the development of the economy. A caricature of a market economy cannot give workers effective decision-making powers over an economy. At the other extreme, a 'national plan' run purely by a small circle of bureaucrats at the top, as well as being unacceptable to the democratic aspirations of the British labour movement, is also economic nonsense in an advanced, highly complex industrial system. The consumer, although having no formal industrial rights, has a vital part to play in exercising controls over prices, quality and choice. Indeed the election of consumer committees at all stages of price and production determination would help to direct industry to the service of the community. The impetus that a nationalised, planned economy would provide to the expansion of consumer industries makes vital this type of full democratic participation in decision-making by both workers and consumers not only for the democratic, but in the economic interests, of the public.

A central planning medium needs the democratic participation of works committees and consumers, as well as specialist advice. Communication in industry in national, as well as plant planning, is a necessity. Ideas, aspirations and intentions need to have full access and be encouraged upward, whilst explanations, snags and problems should move downward for discussion and the creation of an informed working populace. The works committees, rising through industry to national planning, need the safeguards of full political democracy in order to discuss and decide upon alternative plans for economic and structural development. Even where there is full workers' control in the industrial plants, workers will be left in a purely passive executive position if they cannot effectively discuss, and draw up the central plan itself, and have the opportunity to modify or change it in tune with changing circumstances or needs. Here the element of flexibility becomes all-important.

There must obviously be a recognition that specialists would play an important, and possibly more vital role under a structure of workers' self-management. Staff appointments, carrying such duties as design, experiment and research would remain with a high degree of autonomy in their research. Managers with over-all operative duties could work under the guidance and eventual control of representative bodies of workers, holding the power of appointment, promotion and dismissals. Every workshop or department could elect, by secret ballot, representatives to deal with managerial functions and in turn consult frequently with workers. Large factories might require inter-departmental committees, but for smaller plant, the next stage would probably be factory administration. Administration would embrace different functional divisions, comprising members of primary committees together with consumers. Administrative factory committees could be endowed with power to select managers who in turn would appoint supervisory grades, at least in the initial stages. Representatives from Factory Committees, elected to Industrial Councils could be enabled to work out policies relating to the whole industry, and provide a link with other industries and planning authorities. The necessity for control must be balanced by the freedom which enables individuals to apply their own ideas, while keeping in mind, and making allowances for, the wider needs of the community.

It has often been argued that a centralised planning medium of this character will 'inevitably' lead to a new ruling caste of managers and bureaucrats. This is obviously a point that needs to be carefully examined, in particular to see what safeguards, both organisationally and inherent in the structure of the society itself, would militate against this. Obviously the maintenance of political freedom to democratically discuss conflicting views of planning would be a powerful safeguard. But this by itself is not enough. The trade unions' role in a nationalised economy can also be an important factor in this direction. There is an essential need to preserve trade union independence. The unions must not be directly involved in controlling industry. The value of the unions will lie in their ability to take independent action to redress industrial grievances and act as a media for protection against injustice. Even in the content of a plan, there is scope for unions to act as bargaining agents and to play a role in determining wages.

Institutional checks can be introduced to halt any tendency towards an irresponsible bureaucracy. The right of recall of representatives by the membership and the interchangeability of positions, would go a long way in this direction. However the main check to the growth of administrative autonomy by specialists would be provided by the benefits of a socialised economy itself. It has always been a basic socialist thesis that a planned economy would lay the basis for a tremendous increase in material resources, leaving room not only for a swift reduction in the working day (with the use of automation) but allowing, on the foundations of rapid economic growth, for a great extension in educational facilities. Obviously one cannot induce democratic involvement in industry by a stroke of the pen, but an effective participation needs a technologally educated work force. One cannot afford to examine the viability of workers' self-management in a static sense; technological advance could more than be equalled by cultural advance through the growth not only of administrative experience but of vastly improved educational resources. A reduction in the working day to allow time for study, would greatly accelerate this process.

Workers already have the knowledge necessary to effectively increase this country's material resources. We have probably the most industrially experienced work-force in the world. But why should workers bring forward constructive ideas for the efficiency of a plant if it means their employers' gain and with the possibility of their work mates being made redundant as a result? Democratic self-management of industry by the workers themselves would release the long dammed up potential of the worker's hard-won experience. They would see that their creative ideas and suggestions would work, purely and simply for *their* benefit, and for the benefit of the community. This provides the basis for a new psychological attitude towards work, and thereby a raising of both cultural and material levels.

The British Labour Movement has the industrial and organisational experience of generations behind it. We can learn from the experience of other countries that have undergone a transition to the beginnings of a socialist society. And we can remember that as a highly advanced country, with such a strong working-class movement, such a transition can be accomplished more swiftly and easily in Britain. It can genuinely lead to the development of workers' control in industry and politics. We have the opportunity and the potential to make realisable the old socialist aspiration of a society geared, not to the exploitation of man by man, but simple administration by free men over the material abundance of the World.

Hugh Scanlon

31st March 1968

PUBLICATIONS OF THE INSTITUTE FOR WORKERS' CONTROL

PAMPHLET SERIES

1. The Way Forward for Workers' Control — Hugh Scanlon 1/6
2. Productivity Bargaining — Tony Topham 1/6
4. Opening the Books — M. Barratt Brown 1/6
5. The Labour Party's Plans for Industrial Democracy — Ken Coates & Tony Topham 1/6
11. Ten Essays — Antonio Gramsci 1/6
12. The Dockers' Next Step — Hull & London Dock Workers' Control Group 2/6
13. Four Steps to Progress (Workers' Control and the Buses) — Jack Ashwell 2/6
14. The 'Big Flame' and What is the IWC? — M. Barratt Brown and Ken Coates 9d
15. The Law versus the Unions — Ken Coates and Tony Topham 1/6
16. Job Evaluation and Workers' Control — Ray Collins 1/6
17. GEC - EE Workers' Takeover — 2/-
18. A Hope for the Miners? — John Hughes 6d
19. Bertrand Russell and Industrial Democracy — Ken Coates, Lawrence Daly, Bill Jones and Bob Smillie 1/6
20. Farmworkers' Control — Nick Hillier 1/6
21. Problems of Trade Union Democracy — Richard Fletcher 2/-
22. Workers' Control and the Transnational Company — Hugh Scanlon 1/6

BOOKS

Industrial Democracy and Canadian Labour — 15/-
How and Why Industry must be Democratised —
Papers and proceedings of the 1968 Workers' Control Conference
    Edited by Ken Coates and Wyn Williams
    Hardback 32/6   Paperback 15/-
Democracy in the Motor Industry — Edited by Ken Coates 6/-
Can The Workers Run Industry? — Edited by Ken Coates 8/6
The Debate on Workers' Control
    Bert Ramelson, Ken Coates, Tony Topham, Charlie Swain & Bill Jones 6/-
Democracy on the Docks — Edited by Tony Topham 10/-
Trade Union Register — Edited by Ken Coates, Tony Topham,
(1969 and 1970)   Michael Barratt Brown 20/- each

THE INSTITUTE PUBLISHES A QUARTERLY BULLETIN
Single Issues 5/-   Subscription for six issues 30/-

ALSO AVAILABLE:
Badges — "Workers' Control" — 1/- each
Posters — "Eighth National Conference on Workers' Control" — 9/- Doz

from IWC, 45 GAMBLE STREET, FOREST ROAD WEST, NOTTINGHAM

Printed by The Partisan Press Ltd. T.U. Nottm.

Tony Topham

PRODUCTIVITY BARGAINING AND WORKERS' CONTROL

The Institute for Workers' Control

Pamphlet Series No. 2   One Shilling and Sixpence

Productivity Bargaining and Workers' Control

Tony Topham

Introduction

These notes aim only to summarise some of the recent trends which are apparent in the field of productivity bargaining. There is now a substantial body of experience in the trade union movement of this technique of neo-capitalist management, and a revealing literature which has been inspired by it, (notably some publications of the Prices and Incomes Board and the Royal Commission) all of which require more detailed documentary treatment. It is hoped that the workers' control campaign and its publications will produce further work on the subject, in the form of practical guide-lines for workers who are confronted with the problems of productivity bargaining. This service is urgently needed: as the workers accumulate experience and awareness of the snares and traps of productivity bargaining, these should be disseminated widely in the movement. Our aim should be nothing less than a coherent and co-ordinated counter-strategy to the techniques of management and the state, which through the Prices and Incomes Board and the Ministry of Labour, and with the aid of some academics who work for the Royal Commission, is hard at work providing a guide-line service for the employers. Most of what these bodies have published on productivity bargaining takes the form of instructions, hints, or do-it-yourself handbooks, addressed directly to managements. A coherent plan runs through their publications. It is to use productivity bargaining to destroy workers' controls on the shop-floor, to limit or reduce wage-costs in the interests of higher profitability, and to establish greater managerial authority over the use of labour. This statement may be easily verified by readers who care to study:—

1) *Productivity Agreements*, Report No. 36 of the Prices and Incomes Board, Cmnd. 3311, June 1967.

and 2) *Research Papers, No. 4*
on a) Productivity Bargaining
and b) Restrictive Labour Practices.
published by the Royal Commission on Trade Unions and Employers' Associations. H.M.S.O. 1967.

For the moment, the following points require the urgent attention of the trade unions.

a) The Effect of Productivity Bargaining on Wages

There is no final evidence that productivity bargaining improves the relative position of workers affected by them, nor any proof that the standards of life of the working class as a whole will benefit from its adoption. Whilst productivity in manufacturing industry rose by 5·9 per cent last year, average weekly earnings rose by only 5·3 per cent. During the same period, prices rose by 2·5 per cent. Price increases are being deliberately allowed to rise, whilst wage control in many forms (including productivity bargains) is being tightened. No concrete evidence could be found by the Prices and Incomes Board (Report No. 36) that productivity bargains had led to price reductions, or even stability. Some workers obtain big wage increases from productivity bargains, whilst others directly involved, have experienced wage *cuts* from such deals. This can have disastrous effects in dividing workers against one another, as in the case of the Power Loading Agreement in the mining industry. In defending some wage increases under productivity bargaining, the Prices and Incomes Board Report and the Royal Commission paper point to savings in the total wages *bill* which follows from economies in labour use. They also argue that productivity bargaining reduces the demand for labour and hence the pressure for general wage increases. Furthermore, it is often found that whilst wage *rates* may be increased by a productivity bargain, the loss of overtime or bonus payments which are often eliminated, will leave *earnings* relatively unchanged. In the famous Fawley Oil Refinery case, the Esso Company reassured the Royal Commission about the "dangers" that productivity bargaining would stimulate wage claims. The company carried out a survey of eight industries in the (Southampton) region of the Fawley Refinery, four years after their productivity deal. They found that the oil industry had the second highest hourly rates of pay, but its total earnings in relation to hours worked were the lowest of the eight, and its total earnings were sixth out of the eight! In British Rail's new Grading Agreement, (an elaborate industry-level productivity bargain) the total increase in the wage bill is to be a mere three-and-a-half per cent. In the maximum case, an increase of 29/- for some lower grades is offered, whilst for signalmen at present on £17-11-0 no wage increase at all is forthcoming.

The Prices and Incomes Board delights particularly to point out that, in many cases, higher wages paid under a productivity bargain *would have had to be paid anyway*, as a "conventional" wage increase because of the market or bargaining situation of the industry or plant concerned. The management gains from productivity bargaining, in other words, were partly obtained with extra labour costs which were already discounted.

Trade unions and shop stewards must be more vigilant about this basic aspect of productivity bargaining. They should calculate expected conventional wage gains first and demand that those be paid as pre-requisite for commencing a productivity bargain. They should constantly examine the effects of lost overtime and bonus, and insist upon money being involved in the negotiations *at every stage*. (A favourite device of mangement is to defer the wage offer part of the bargain *until after* agreement has been reached on a wide range of labour practice changes. At that point, it becomes a matter of "take-it-or-leave-it". A feeling that they have 'sold cheap' is common amongst workers after the completion of a deal).

In a climate of nil norm and restrictive legislation, trade unions have sometimes assumed that they could get round the wage freeze by productivity bargaining. "We went in for it because this was the only way to get an increase", is a typical kind of remark from trade union officials and shop stewards. One may have some sympathy with this view, and certainly in some cases the workers themselves, seeing apparent gains made in a neighbouring factory, have sometimes pressed officials into productivity bargaining. But the evidence suggests that the wage gains through productivity bargaining are often illusory, extremely moderate. partial, and temporary and are often made at the expense of fellow-workers. The longer-term effect of a productivity bargain may well (as at Fawley) lead to a relative *decline* of the wage level, as managerial control is permanently strengthened, and local shop steward initiative is weakened by the institutional changes built in to the agreement. (See below).

It looks as though the attempt, by trade unions, to get round the incomes policy by exploiting its productivity clauses, will prove to have been a failure, and that a response based on a more thorough-going critique of the basic concepts of that policy must be produced.

b) Effects on Employment

Unemployment, in January 1968, was 30·8 per cent higher than in January 1967. We have noted that in the same period, manufacturing productivity rose by 5·9 per cent. Productivity bargaining was being pursued throughout this time. Of course the overall cause of rising unemployment has been government economic policy, and is not directly attributed to the effects of productivity bargaining. However, there is no doubt whatsoever that one of the basic aims of such bargains is to economise in labour usage, and that the result in almost all cases is to restrict the demand for labour in the local and regional markets affected by particular deals. Some productivity bargains contain a "no redundancy" clause, and it is obviously one minimum safeguard which unions should insist upon. (It is not always done however: the British Rail flexible grading scheme will make 8,500 railwaymen redundant, in addition to the 12,000 who are to lose jobs because of rail closures this year.) A "no redundancy" clause, however, may disguise the fact that job opportunities are being *reduced*. Whilst the sectional interests of workers on the site are apparently protected, the effect is to worsen the local unemployment situation. This, in its turn, eventually weakens the bargaining power of the workers directly involved in the deal. The "no redundancy" clause itself may therefore be vulnerable; militant action *in defence of an agreement* is rendered less effective if the local dole queue is a long one. Workers and their union representatives must develop a strategy which takes into account the whole local and regional labour market. A "no redundancy" clause at plant level is not enough. Estimates should be made of the *loss of job opportunities* entailed in any employer's productivity or "flexibility" proposals, and demands must be made for guaranteed *additional* employment in the locality or region, *before* the deal is negotiated. This brings into view the whole question of trade union pressure (through Trades Councils, shop steward committees, etc.) upon the present government's regional unemployment policies.

We have argued above that over-enthusiastic trade union response to productivity deals should be tempered, in the light of their dubious effects upon wages. The same conclusion can be drawn from an examination of their effects upon employment.

c) Effects upon Workers' Control

A general recognition of the great potential danger to trade union and shop steward authority, which is implicit in all productivity bargaining, has recently been forthcoming from the leaderships of the two largest trade unions. Hugh Scanlon makes the point in his *New Left Review* interview. (*N.L.R.*, No. 46, Nov-Dec. 1967, pages 8-9)

> " . . . All my life I've attributed most of the ills of the engineering industry to an iniquitous piece-work system. Yet the moment anyone wants to do away with it, we fight with all the vigour we can command to retain it, and correctly so.
> Because with piece-work you have the man on the shop-floor determining how much effort they will give for a given amount of money. In other words there is a mutually agreed contract between operators and management's representatives. Now, with the introduction of new ideas like measured day work, you have a fixed wage and the only question is — how much work you will do for that fixed wage. This is a developing phenomenon which is meeting with resentment . . . I would resist to the utmost . . . a scheme that does not contain the fact of mutuality within it. For what is important . . . is that once the piecework bargain is struck, the worker can work at the speed he chooses."

Writing in the T.&G.W.U. Journal *The Record*, in January 1968, that union's Education Secretary, Tony Corfield, discusses the switch of management initiative from piece-work and incentive systems, (developed in the forties and fifties) to measured day work systems. He adds:

> " ... it is essential that our shop stewards appreciate what they are giving up when management propose going over to fixed day wages. The loss may not be in earning capacity. The change may involve a loss of workshop participation and control over the payments system."

The shop stewards at B.M.C. have demonstrated their own clear understanding of the significance of measured day work. (See *New Deal or New Fetters?* published by the Oxford Liason Committee for the Defence of Trade Unions, 1967).

In their pamphlet on measured day work at B.M.C., the stewards show the contrast between gains made by workers under piece-work systems, (as at B.M.C. in the past) and day wage methods (as at Fords and Vauxhall) and they comment:

> "It is the strength of our shop stewards backed by our readiness to take militant action that has won us our present wage levels. Much of the power of shop stewards comes from their negotiations over piece rates and lieu rates. By doing away with these negotiations the B.M.C. bosses hope to be able to break our factory union organisation.
> Once we lose control over wage rates the bosses hope they can determine the line speed and the labour loading, i.e. the number of men engaged on a particular job. At Vauxhalls the line is constantly being speeded up as a result of measured day work and there is a higher degree of labour mobility within the factory. Workers, including stewards, are constantly being pushed around from one job to another. This way they hope to isolate potential 'trouble-makers' and prevent us getting together with our mates and doing something about it."

Measured Day Work is one of the important devices often incorporated in a productivity bargain, along with flexibility of labour, abolition or curtailment of overtime, etc., which have the effect of weakening shop stewards' controls and sanctions on the job. As Scanlon says, piece rates involve "the principle of mutuality" —they are *bargaining* for with the union or stewards in an independent position. Management is increasingly alive to the chance of seizing *unilateral* control over jobs, speeds, and conditions of work, in their drive to eliminate the *contractual* element in local bargaining. Consider for example, the following clause in Priestman's (Engineering) Ltd., deal, signed with the A.E.U. and N.U.G.M.W. in 1967.

"**Measured Day Work**

The Management will set times or 'norms' on all jobs, where possible, at which an average man working at average speed should complete a task. A man whose times are consistently in excess of the norm time by 10% or more will be investigated to find out:—

    (a) is the norm correct.
    (b) has he a personal problem
    (c) is the job suitable for him.
    (d) is he not making the necessary effort.

A man who consistently completes his task in less than the norm by 10% or more) will be regarded as having increased productivity and will be considered for up-grading or promotion when a vacancy arises. It is in the spirit of this agreement that, with the removal of individual incentive payments, men who have the ability to beat the norm for a job will continue to do so as any falling off of effort will jeopardize the future productivity bonus."

This at least has the negative merit of being such a direct assault upon workers' controls, that it is easily recognisable as such, and the appropriate moral drawn from it. A more subtle undermining of the steward's position takes the form of an attempt to incorporate them in management activity. Some productivity deals have taken up to a year to negotiate, with management-steward meetings occuring several times a week, interspersed with week-end conferences in club-like surroundings. Most stewards are acutely aware of the nature of the persuasion to which they are subjected, but some must undoubtedly be swayed by the whole solemn aura of the process, and become totally absorbed in the pure *process* of rationalisation, ending up with a high degree of commitment to the *"success"* of the scheme on which they have lavished so much time and care. In these circumstances, it is not surprising to learn that the Royal Commission is contemplating a series of recommendations to raise the status of shop stewards, and to increase the number of full-time convenors, jointly paid by unions and management, and carefully trained in the correct procedures and attitudes. Nor is it surprising to learn that in some firms, a new 'unofficial' shop steward system has emerged, as the process of incorporation has reached such proportions that the stewards are finally separated from their constituents' interests. (We should note that the Prices and Incomes Board found that whilst union officials were almost all favourable to productivity bargaining, the response of shop stewards was more often critical.)

Another variant on this development is the management offer of a permanent 'pay and productivity committee' to police the agreement after it has been signed. Now obviously the *follow-up* to a productivity bargain is most important for the workers, for upon it can depend whether management achieves *in practice* the restoration of managerial control which it has striven to establish on paper. The interpretation of agreements has traditionally been an area of *bargaining*, supported in the last resort by the industrial action which unions may take, or which unofficial pressure may demand. But in some recent cases, management's version of the 'productivity committee' has been that it should be *advisory*, confining itself to making "recommendations" about the application of the deal. Clearly, to accept such a position would entail a major set-back in the whole post-war development of workers' controls on the shop floor.

The demand, which has been often expressed in recent literature, for the opening of the books as a union condition for productivity bargaining, has reached a great number of shop stewards, and is present in a partial form in the official programme of some unions, as well as in the Labour Party Report on Industrial Democracy. (June 1967, price 1/6). However, there is as yet little understanding of how this demand should be used in practice, and some managements have successfully anticipated it by offering to the stewards their own edited versions of the secrets of their company. The limited and highly dubious value of such offers is clear from such incidents as the aircraft companies' fiddling of the books in government contracts. It is also obvious from the evasive and utterly incomplete review of the "Net Gains" made by companies through productivity bargains, which is offered by the Royal Commission paper, and by the Prices and Incomes Board (Report No. 36, pages 16-24). It is not unlikely that the Prices and Incomes Board knows more about this than it is prepared to publish; in that same report it recommends that management should be discreetly selective about the commercial secrets revealed to unions in productivity bargaining. (See Coates and Topham on the Labour Party Report on Industrial Democracy). Academic researchers into industry, leave alone government bodies and trade unions, are familiar with the problem of being granted access to company accounts *only* on condition that they respect the confidences thus obtained.

The response of shop stewards to this situation must be one of total scepticism in the face of management's figures, and a pursuit of the subject through to the very vitals of the financial system. It must include an insistence that trade union accountants be given unlimited access to company records on depreciation and reserves, which must be checked against the direct eye-witness knowledge of the stewards. It must include the preservation of the full rights of stewards to report back all their findings, without restraint or commitment to company secrecy. If necessary, the bargaining must be suspended or terminated in the absence of satisfactory access to company secrets.

Conclusion.

These considerations can never be finally resolved at the local, plant level. What is required is a ground-swell of demands, aimed at placing the employers and the state on the defensive in this matter and raising the political question of *accountability* to the centre of our campaign. (See Michael Barratt-Brown's paper 'Open the books'.) In this way we shall expose the basic purpose of productivity bargaining which is, from the point of view of the state and the employers, to reduce labour costs and to maintain or increase the level of profit. For a trade union movement whose long term aspirations include an assault on the gross inequities in income distribution between work and property, such a purpose cannot command its support or acquiescence, particularly if, as these notes have argued, the process also involves the undermining of basic trade union bargaining power and independence. At a time when trade union leadership, impelled by the dissatisfaction of its members, is timorously withdrawing from consensus relations at the national level, it must not seek a new and equally false haven by encouraging consensus at the plant level.

The shop stewards for their part, must base their resistance to consensus on a coherent strategy which, starting with plant level demands for accountability, reaches out to challenge the widest aspects of managerial and state controls. They might begin, to cite just a few instances, by demanding explanations of the following company statements to the Royal Commission (pages 36-37 of Research Paper No. 4).

1. **Dunlop Rubber** "accurate measurement of net saving in the cost of the product should provide the basis of the bargain. Unless a productivity bargain yields a true saving in the FULL product cost there is no advantage to the enterprise." (no other details given.)

2. **Esso** " . . . is satisfied that the agreements it has been able to reach so far were well work making in financial terms." (No other details given.)

3. **Mobil Oil:** their distribution agreement "will mean more efficient and less costly operation . . ." (No other details given.)

4. **Petrochemicals:** ". . . we are unable to give details of our calculations on the savings we hope to make as a result of adopting flexible working at Carrington . . . In a capital-intensive industry whose products have suffered constant erosion on price as the result of national and international competition we would not have committed ourselves to our present course if we were not

satisfied that it would represent a continuum of the containment improvement in net manufacturing costs from which we have benefited since the early part of 1963." (No other details given.)

5. **Steel Company of Wales:** ". . . a productivity bargain in which, through better use of resources, everybody gains, is psychologically very good for management. The sense of incurring a loss is avoided; on the contrary not only its profitability but also its control of operations will have been improved." (No other details given.)

After all that, we can perhaps agree with the laconic conclusion of the Royal Commission paper itself. "It is unfortunate that more precise figures are not available."

The advanced sections of British management, assisted by the state, have now acquired considerable expertise in productivity bargaining. Typically, managers now take considerable time and care in the preparation of a deal. Before they ever invite the participation of shop stewards and unions, they have spent perhaps months in behind-the-scenes discussion amongst themselves, fixing their goals, planning their strategy, re-organising the "management team". In the process, they have acquired a new ambition, a new philosophy of managerial control. As a result, the stewards and unions start the bargaining in an inferior position, unprepared, and on the defensive. Even the best and most militant unionists are at a disadvantage in this situation. By giving attention to some of the points outlined in these notes, the worst consequences may be mitigated, and there are doubtless numerous other counter-strategies which have been developed and which remain to be uncovered and disseminated in the movement. But the workers remain in a position of defence, faced with a bargain which is fundamentally about managerial control.

A major breakthrough could be achieved if the advanced sectors of the shop stewards movement took a leaf out of the tactical book of management, and *reversed the whole process*. Instead of a productivity bargain, why not a "control bargain"? The first stages would be conducted by the stewards and unions themselves, in a particular firm or plant or industry. Detailed discussion and careful preparations would be conducted, setting the goals and the minimum demands. What aspects of workers' control do we want to advance, what areas of managerial authority do we wish to challenge and acquire for the workers, what reductions in top executive salaries do we seek and what restrictions on information do we wish to challenge? What wage structure and overall wage increase will we settle for? What research into the firm's profits, structure, monopoly links, and alliance with the state, is needed?

After the goals are settled — a process which must involve a thoroughly democratic debate for the whole trade union membership in the firm or industry — the demands should be presented. The initiative rests now with the workers. Their demands must be explained and disseminated throughout the labour movement; they are utterly reasonable, for they begin from a premise of *equality of status* between the contending sides of industry. They aim to achieve, however, a dominance for the *majority* in industry; the workers by hand and by brain. (Attention should be given to the role of the white-collar workers, particularly the draughtsmen and technicians, not only because these are organised in militant unions, but because they normally have access to specialised knowledge of a firm's affairs.) The bargain then proceeds, until or unless the proposals are rejected by the representatives of the employers — i.e. the representatives of the small, wealthy minority in our society, which "owns" the firm or industry.

Imagine such a bargain. Imagine what happens if the workers' proposals are rejected. Assuming a real industrial democracy, with complete equality with management, what would the workers do? What do the employers' representatives do in today's circumstances? If the trade union refuses to meet them on their productivity proposals, management responds by predicting and threatening redundancies and dismisals, or reduced wages.

If the shoe was on the other foot, how many redundancies amongst directors would the workers decide upon? How, indeed, could workers continue to maintain production in the face of such stubborn refusal to co-operate on their proposals?

It all sounds very fanciful. But this, brothers, is how management and the state normally behaves towards you, in *their* industrial democracy".

Summary

1, Productivity bargaining is not a universal substitute for a challenge to wage restraint. Gains in wage rates are often offset by loss of overtime and bonus earnings. Initiative over *future* wage increases may be lost to the stewards and unions.

2. In the absence of full employment and an expanding labour market, productivity bargaining indirectly adds to the unemployment problem, by limiting or reducing future demand for labour.

3. The aim of productivity bargaining, in the eyes of the state and employers, is to achieve wage control and higher profitability by undermining workers' controls at the plant level. Amongst the techniques used are measured day work, and the incorporation

of the shop steward system into elaborate patterns of negotiation and co-operation.

4. The details of company gains from productivity bargaining are deliberately withheld from the stewards, the unions, and official enquiries.

5. A satisfactory trade union response to these findings requires:—

- a) a higher *monetary* price on productivity deals
- b) safeguards against the fall in demands for labour
- c) the defence and advance of worker controls at plant level
- d) the co-ordination of these positions into a total strategy which can enforce accountability upon industry and the state
- e) the process of productivity bargaining should be stood on its head, and the initiative for a 'control bargain' seized by the workers.

March 1968

Labour and Sterling

Michael Barratt-Brown

Published by The Institute for Workers Control

Pamphlet Series No. 3   One Shilling & Sixpence

Michael Barratt Brown

Labour and Sterling

In any survey of the world system in which a Labour Government in Britain has had to work since 1964 we must start from the fact that Britain has become a rather weak member in the second rank of capitalist powers increasingly dominated by United States capital but still dominating the economies of a group of small and far less developed countries. Once the workshop and then the banker for the greatest empire in the world, British capitalism had for long tried to reconcile the roles of banker and trader. For the banker, the rate of return is the crucial question; for the trader, the growth of his trade. Since the war the City has flourished and industry has declined. Sterling devaluation spells the collapse of a long struggle to revive London's banking role but it spells more than that.

The Crisis of the Sterling Bankers

Through the whole period from 1955 high interest rates (never below 4½ %) were funds to the City of London which could then be invested abroad for even higher long term return. By 1960 the outward flow of long term capital exceeded £400 million with only £150 million flowing from outside. The gap was plugged as usual by short-term borrowing.

Mr. Heath claims that there was an aggregate surplus on the Balance of Payments during the years of Tory rule. There was on current account a small average annual surplus but on capital account there was a large annual deficit. We may summarise the balance of payments on average and in the three years of heaviest deficit between 1952 and 1965.

	Annual Average 1952-64	1955	1960	1964	1965-66
Balance on Goods	-177	-313	-408	-543	-216
Balance on Services	+190	+129	+174	+167	+176
Net Property Income	+282	+174	+242	+416	+409
Government Spending	-239	-138	-283	-433	-453
Net Capital Account	-165	-122	-192	-368	-174
Deficit met by Short-Term Money	110	277	467	761	258

It can be seen that while on average over the period of Tory rule there was just a balance of goods and services taken together and property income from overseas just exceeded Government spending, the net outflow of long term capital had still to be largely covered by short-term money.

In the years of maximum deficit, however, all three of the major deficit items grew – the deficit on exports of goods, the increase in government overseas spending, nearly two-thirds of which is military, and the net outflow of capital. Although the average annual increase of borrowing at £110 million may not seem large, the figures of nearly £300 million, nearly £500 million and finally nearly £800 million in the deficit years show the gathering seriousness of the crisis. There are thus two parts to the problem – first the worsening imbalance in export and import of goods, which in the three worst years accounts for more than half of the total deficit. Second, there is the steady increase of short-term debt by over £100 million every year. These are the two parts of the balance of payments crisis that faced the Labour Government. The short term loans could easily be withdrawn and were in fact withdrawn at the first whisper of doubt about the possibility of maintaining the value of sterling in relation to other currencies. What could the Government do?

Let us set down the Country's financial Assets and Liabilities side by side as they stood in December 1964. There was an overall positive balance of over £200 million, but the short term balance was in deficit, even though, it must be remembered, this was after borrowing nearly £900 million from the International

Item		Assets		Liabilities	
Long Term					
Inter-Govt. Loans		817		1648	
Private Investment		9420		4075	
of which:	Portfolio	3600		1500	
	Companies Direct (excl. oil)	4520		1825	
	Oil Companies	1300		750	
Long Term Total			10250	5950	= Net 4300
Short Term					
Trade Credit		691		142	
Banking	– Sterling currency	1178		4634	
	– Non-Sterling	1626		1856	
I.M.F. Account		695		881	
Government Portfolio		470		---	
Gold and Reserves		827		---	
Short Term Total		**5475**		**7500**	**= Net -1125**
Long Term and Short Term		**15725**		**13450**	**= Net 2275**

Monetary Fund. The Government had another £470 million in its portfolio of securities, a large part of which could be – and were in the event – disposed of; but the short term deficit remained and it only needed a swing from credit to debit of the traders, who buy and sell sterling from day to day for paying their bills, to start a further run on the pound. Much of the sterling currency debt of the London banks is held officially by foreign governments as reserves for their currencies and they were unlikely to try suddenly to change these from sterling to other currencies; but non-governmental holders would certainly try to get out of sterling in a major crisis.

The obvious course for the government would appear to have been to realise some of the long-term assets that have been built up overseas and, in this way, to meet the short term debt. But here there was a snag. These assets were largely in private hands. Moreover, two-thirds were directly invested by companies, including the oil companies, in subsidiaries and branches overseas. Nevertheless, £3600 million were in private portfolios, that is investments by persons and institutions in companies abroad; and these could have been nationalised and sold to meet the debt. In fact discussions are now being held by the Government with Investment Trusts with a view to persuading them to realise some of their overseas holdings and pass the dollars to the Government. Such voluntary methods of realising private assets abroad are very unlikely to be adequate. Yet it is clear for the Labour Government to have made compulsory purchases would have been raised the whole question of the confidence of the City and of the foreign bankers. Even if foreign exchange controls could have been imposed quickly enough and foreign assets could have been frozen, the process of Government intervention could not have stopped there. The demand of the Left for nationalising the private foreign portfolio would have required in effect nationalising the whole banking system to prevent wholesale- withdrawals of capital from Britain. Nor could intervention have been stopped at this point. Of course, the withdrawal of capital takes no single piece of machinery or equipment with it, but the short-term effect on trade credit would have required Government control over foreign trade as well.

There is an evident conflict here between the City's banking role and the needs of British industry; but the conflict lies in the whole structure by Government control of foreign trade and finance, there would not only be a loss of some £250 million a year - the City's contribution from banking, insurance and other services to the Balance of Payments – but huge problems of restructuring would still face British industry. For it is the City bankers who finance British industry both at home and in their operations overseas but it is increasingly British industry itself that requires the outflow of capital each years, which we have seen be so large a part of the cause of the balance of payments deficits. To compete with their opposite numbers in the United States and West Germany, British firms have had both to increase their hold on sources of oil and other industrial raw materials and to establish subsidiaries in their competitor's own markets overseas.

The international company is the driving force of modern capitalism. To succour its vast operations there must be a surplus on the balance of payments in the country from where it originates. Such a surplus can only be found either from a direct surplus of the home country's exports over imports, or from the reparation of earning from overseas operations or, as we have seen, from short term borrowing. The very increase in the operations of overseas subsidiaries may tend to reduce direct exports by UK companies and their earnings overseas may be required for reinvestment overseas. If this happens, short term borrowing must increasingly be relied upon.

This is what happened in Britian in the last fifteen years, but it would be missing an important aspect of the truth if we failed to recognise that the trick – the bankers' confidence trick of borrowing short and lending long- very neatly came off. If we combine the capital account and the property income and government accounts in the balance of payments, that is by separating these from the private good and services accounts, there really was a capital and income balance; but it was not large enough to pay for the military and other government overseas expenditure that such a balance is involved. Let us take three periods since 1958 and set down side by side the flows each way of income from property and investment both from ploughing back of that income and from fresh capital (plus = flow in to Britain; minus = flow out).

Flows in £ms	Year 1958 (Income Investment)		Average 1959-64 (Income Investment)		Average 1965-66 (Income Investment)	
British Income from Abroad and Investment Going Abroad	+684	-294	+739	-342	+970	-412
Foreign Income from Britain and Investment In Britain	-389	+104	-435	+195	-562	+212
Income and Investment Balance	+295	-190	+304	-140	+408	-200
Government Transfers	+3	-77	0	-107	0	-155
Military Expenditure	+52	-173	+38	-224	+25	-295
Combined Balance	-96		-136		-217	

The overall figures for investment include not only Government loans to foreign countries but also the repayment by the Government of foreign loans made to Britain. Without the suspensions of repayments on the American loan in 1965 there would have been an even worse balance in the last two years. The other element in the apparent improvement was the sale by the Government of some £200 million of its own portfolio of foreign investment in those years.

The fact must here be faced that even if the overseas military expenditure had been sharply cut back by the Government, it would have been necessary to increase the item of Government transfers. For these are grants made to ex-colonial lands, not only to replace their dependence on British military expenditure as in Malta or Aden but to help finance their economic development in such a way as to encourage them to go on buying British goods.

This analysis of the role of capital movements in the sterling crisis indicates at once the difficulties facing a government that was committed to remaining within the boundaries of the mixed economy. It also precisely illustrates the position of British capital. Since the war British capital investment has been built up overseas not only in the old fields of oil and raw materials, but even more today in the new fields of manufacturing plants, mainly in the other advances industrial lands and even in the U.S.A. By these means British capitalism tries to retain its dominating role. For many years, even after the war, the resources for its export of capital were found from the earnings of the colonial lands themselves, which had by virtue of membership of the sterling area to bank in London. The self-governing lands spent their own earnings, but the earnings of the colonies could be used to balance Britain's deficits. Now only Malaysia and the oil states remain to supply the resources for the City's long-term investments. Hence the need to preserve the imperial role East of Suez at so great a cost. The cost of course is paid by the taxpayer; the benefits reaped by the investors. To preserve British capitalism and the imperial role the Government was in fact forced to borrow again and again from the United States and the other capitalist bankers. Devaluation of the Pound in November 1967 marked the final downgrading of British capitalism from the first rank to at best the leader to the client states. The confidence trick could be maintained no longer. It is because some businessmen thought that a Tory Government might have kept it up longer that anger has mounted against the Labour Government. But the fundamental facts underlying the crisis of sterling are to be found in the interrelationship between the banking role of the City and the decline of British industry.

The Decline of British Industry

In 1950 British industry was not backward except in relation to the United States. British exporters still provided over a quarter of the manufactured exports of industrial lands, nearly as much as did the United States. By 1964 the British share had been halved, while U.S and West Germany exporters were providing over 20% each. In the decade after 1955 exports of British manufactures rose by about 3% a year whilst imports of foreign manufacturers rose annually by 9%. The result is that by 1967 manufactured imports into Britain were equal to three-quarters of manufactured exports; imports of machinery and transport equipment to half of the exports of these items – and these are Britain's stock in trade par excellence.

What has happened? It is not difficult to see from the available figures that investment in new equipment has proceeded faster on the Continent than in Britain. With productivity rising in the UK manufacturing industry very much more slowly by 37% between 1955 and 1966) than elsewhere (50% in the US and 67% up West Germany), increased wage costs per unit of output we're pushing at British prices. Indeed, British firms which export on average nearly a fifth of their output has been forced to squeeze their profit margins in the exports market. This can be seen from the fact that whereas UK manufactured export prices rose by 27% between 1955 and 1966 (well ahead of the figures for all other advanced industrial countries of around 15%, this rise was much less than the rise over the same period in all home costs (36%).

Nor only were British manufacturers becoming uncompetitive but it was evident that British capital exports were failing to obtain similar rates to return to those of their competitors, at least to those of the US. We may follow E.V. Morgan's figures of Net Income/ Assets Ratios for UK and US Companies in the five years 1958-62.

Where Invested	Rates of Return	
	U.K. Companies	U.S Companies
Domestic Rates in U.K.	7.8	---
in U.S.A.	---	9.1
Foreign Investment – All Countries	7.9	10.2
in U.S.A.	6.6	---
in U.K.	---	12.5
in E.E.C.	8.9	14.2
in Australia	7.2	11.5
in India	8.8	11.9
Foreign Investment – All Industries	7.9	10.2
in Mining	12.1	10.9
in Manufacture	7.4	10.1
in Other	7.7	14.1

It will be seen that the rates of return on US capital were higher both in domestic investment and in foreign investment than those on UK capital; in addition, the rate of return on US capital invested abroad was higher than on US capital invested at home, whilst there was little difference in the two rates on UK capital. Rates of return on British capital at home were declining steadily throughout the 1950s. Between 1954-1958 net income as a percentage of net assets for quoted companies in manufacturing fell from 19% to 15%; there was a slight recovery in 1960 but by 1962 the figure was 12%. In the engineering industry the fall between 1954 and 1962 was from 21% to 11% an in vehicles from 25% to 10%.

British industry was evidently caught in a pincers movement. US and German firms were not only challenging the profits of British firms operating overseas; they were also challenging them in their own home market. United States firms were investing in their British subsidiaries throughout the 1950's at a rate of at least £100 million a year and the resulting population was yielding a rate of return on capital twice as high as that enjoyed by British firms.

The power of United States capital depends on its enormous technological superiority. To compete in the world market any other producer requires lower levels of wages until his technology catches up. If his technology improves haltingly and productivity is stagnant or rises slowly, not only are wages threatened by so is his whole competitive position. And if only some producers in any country improve their technology so that their higher productivity allows higher wages but some industrial sectors or parts of the country lag behind, the tension between different wage levels becomes serious. If this happens in a situation where there is a tendency for imports to rise faster than exports, then wage increases in some sectors, plus credit released for electoral purposes, can easily push overall demand ahead of productivity and pull in huge waves of additional imports.

This brings us to a further problem facing British capitalism at the end of the 1950s. The power of British trade unions in conditions of full employment to raise wages ahead of productivity must here be noted. In the late 1940s and early 1950s real wages undoubtedly lagged behind the rises in output per man. Profits boomed. From 1954 to 1960 hourly earnings in manufacturing industry in Britain discounted for price increases, i.e. real earnings rose ahead of output per man per hour. Profits were reduced. In West Germany and the USA by contrast productivity rose faster than real earnings over these years. Profits in these two countries boomed and investment in new plant and equipment leapt ahead.

Earning and Output Per Man Hour in Manufacturing Industry

U.K.	1953	1960	1963	1966	'66 as % of 1962
Hourly Wage Rates	100	140	162	194	124
Hourly Earnings	100	155	176	220	128
Retail Prices	100	121	133	149	114
Real Earnings	100	128	132	147	112
O.M.H.	100	120	131	147	119
U.S.A.					
Hourly Earnings	100	129	141	153	114
Retail Prices	100	110	115	122	108
Real Earnings	100	117	123	127	105
O.M.H.	100	125	140	154	114
West Germany					
Hourly Earnings	100	158	210	267	137
Retail Prices	100	111	120	132	114
Real Earnings	100	141	275	202	121
O.M.H.	100	142	161	186	123

The problem of rising earnings in relation to productivity was exacerbated for British industry by the nature of the Tory election booms in the "never-had-it-so-good" 1950's. The share of the national income going into private consumption was raised in the boom at the expense of the public services. When the release of credit for private consumption had pulled in excessive imports and upset the balance of payments, a severe check was administered to all economic activity. The result was not only a Stop-Go cycle of current demand but a series of checks to company investment plans. The share of the national product going to new investment was thus held back. We may compare Britain's performance in the 1950's with that of other countries.

Country	Gross Domestic Investment as % of G.N.P.		Rates of Growth O.M.H.	
	Total	Machinery and Equipment Only	Total	Industry
Norway	26.4	15.5	3.2	2.0
Canada	24.8	8.3	2.0	1.7
Netherlands	24.2	11.0	3.7	4.4
West Germany	24.0	11.1	5.3	5.7
Sweden	21.3	7.5	---	---
Italy	20.8	9.0	4.1	5.0
France	19.1	8.1	3.9	4.0
U.S.A.	19.1	7.2	2.1	2.2
Denmark	18.1	9.0	2.3	---
Belgium	16.5	7.3	2.5	3.5
U.K.	15.4	7.4	1.9	2.1

Just as growth is a cumulative process, so is decline. Once the British industrial base at home was weakened by the failure to invest a large enough proportion of the national product in new plant and equipment, exports became less competitive, imports flowed in; when at the same time British capitalism was proceeding to build up its overseas operations and to support these with military bases, the strain on the balance of payments became serious enough. But every new check to growth while the balance was righted – after 1955, after 1960 and again after 1964 – each new wave of short term borrowing from abroad at higher and higher interest rates only worsened the competitive position of industry at home. When demand is held back at home, investment in new plants stop. By contrast the surplus of exports from West Germany made possible continuous growth which created the opportunity for further investments in new plant and so for still more competitive exports until West Germany's payments surplus could easily finance the outflow of West German capital for the foreign operations of West German firms.

Response of British Industry to the Crisis

There can be no doubt that 1960 marked a turning point for British capitalism. Up till then British industry had been shielded by a combination of factors – the slow recovery of the defeated nations, the inflow of public and private capital including not only investments of US firms but the dollar earnings of the Colonies, the fall in import prices, the spending of wartime accumulations of reserves by the developing lands. At the same time the City of London had succeeded in moving very near to full sterling convertibility and in re-establishing itself as the second, if not the first, financial centre of the world. The British balance of payments crisis of 1960 revealed the exposed position of the British economy. West German exports of manufactures had surpassed those of Britain in 1958 while Japan and Italy were steadily increasing their shares. Partly as a result of the recovery of the defeated nations, world prices of food and raw materials were once again rising. The overseas countries of the Sterling Area we rebeginning to run deficits of their own to add to Britain's deficit. The "never-had-it-so-good" pre-election boom provided by the Macmillan Government in 1959, with consumption increased ahead of output, only added the last straw.

The responses of British capitalism to this critical situation can be equally clearly dated from 1960. Some of these may be regarded as deliberately planned, most as the natural reactions of capitalists in a competitive situation. These two obvious competitive reactions were first the sudden increase in mergers and take-overs that can be dated back to 1959 and second, renewed expansion of overseas investment by British Companies.

What resulted from this process or merger and take-over and foreign investment was that the largest companies in Britain achieved an even more dominating position in the economy than before.

If we examine the companies which had achieved a figure of £25 million of net assets by 1963 in the sectors of manufacturing, distribution and construction (excluding oil, shipping and insurance for which similar figures are not available) we obtain the following picture [see next page].

Although the twelve giants have lost some of their dominance, the top 116 had even by 1963 raised their share of all company assets to nearly 60% of the total and had in the process taken 90% of the new capital raised in the previous seven years. The fastest growing third of the top 116 took nearly half the new capital and almost doubled their share of the assets. If we were to include the giant oil and shipping companies, as the lists published by *The Times Review of Industry* do, there is no doubt that we could say that the top 120 companies in

Type of Company (by Asset size in 1963)	Net Assets		Average Income	New Capital raised annually
	1957	1963	1958-63	1958-63
All Quoted Companies (in £m)	10,219	15,640	2386	313
of which (as % of all)				
Top 12 Companies	22	19	19	24
Next 104 Companies	34	40	36	56
Remaining 1800	44	41	45	17
Fastest Growing 42 of the Top 116	11	19	17	45
Top 7 U.S. Companies	3	3.5	4.25	1.75

Britain own a half of all the assets and probably account for nearly two thirds of all home sales; fifty companies including oil and shipping companies account for perhaps half of the sales.

But even these giant firms remain uncompetitive in the world market. It is first of all evident that the seven top United States Companies operating in Britain have a much larger share of the income than of the other large companies. A study of the *Fortune* magazine lists of top companies shows, moreover, that British companies net assets are not smaller on average in most industries (automobiles are the exception) than those of their United States companies. The sales per employee are relatively lower still. In other words the technology of the UK companies is still much behind that of the giant United States companies.

We need now to note the implication of this great concentration of capital in the largest companies which are those that have become more internationalised. First, over a fifth of the annual new British company capital investment (i.e. excluding the investment of foreign company capital in Britain and excluding depreciation provisions) has in recent years been invested outside the country. This is a sum equal to the net annual investment of all the nationalised industries.

Studies made at the Department of Applied Economics in Cambridge have suggested that in 1961 the net worth of overseas subsidiaries and branches was already equal to just under a fifth of the total net worth of all British companies.

Secondly, the result of this great wave of overseas investments is that many of the largest British companies are selling nearly as much in foreign markets as at home not mainly through direct exports but through their subsidiary companies.

A few examples will serve to illustrate the point. They are taken from those amongst the top 100 companies which happen to publish their export and turnover figures by home and overseas markets.

Distribution of Certain Large British Company Sales at Home and Overseas
(in million pounds)

Company	Year	Total Sales	Home Market	Direct Export	Sales from Overseas Subsidiaries
I.C.I.	1963	625	325	115	184
G.K.N.	1966	330	214	22	94
B.I.C.C.	1966	299	155	46	98
English Electric	1966	270	174	47	49
A.E.I.	1966	265	137	48	80
Metal Box	1966	141	96	8	37
G.E.C.	1963	122	85	19	28
Albright & Wilson	1966	96	54	18	24
Reckitt & Colman	1964	96	36	6	54
British Oxygen	1966	95	43	8	44
Glaxo	1966/7	70	24	13	33

It cannot certainly be argued that the exports of such firms are lower than they would be otherwise have been had they not established overseas subsidiaries. The Reddaway Report on the Effects of UK Direct Investment Overseas took a fairly favourable view of the export effect since it seemed likely that in most cases overseas markets would have been lost if subsidiaries had not been established. The picture varies from industry to industry. We have Dunning's estimates (Moorgate and Well Street, Autumn 1966) of the share of exports as a proposition of output in the UK for leading overseas investors and for all companies to judge by.

Industry	Total Exports from U.K. 1964	Exports as % of all firms	Firms U.K. Output for Leading Investors
	£m	%	%
Non-Elect' Engineering	852	29.2	19.2
Vehicles	658	33.4	28.1
Textiles	420	17.7	16.0
Chemicals	412	18.8	13.7
Electrical Engineering	315	19.8	21.7
Food, Drink, Tobacco	251	4.3	15.9
Paper etc.	50	6.1	4.1

Dunning surprisingly draws the conclusion from this Table that the leading investors contribute neither more nor less to export from their output than others. It is hard to see how he reaches this conclusion.

If we take from the *Times* List of the top 300 UK Companies those which publish their turnover and exports sales and compare them with national totals we certainly find that the largest companies make a surprisingly small contribution to exports. While the top 45 companies probably provide nearly a half of all sales at home they provide less than a quarter of all exports.

Thus a listing of the total Assets, Sales and Exports of groups of UK Companies according to their size (figure in £m) reveals the following picture.

Companies by Size	Net Assets	Turnover (incl. overseas)	Exports of goods and services
Top 45 giving turnover figures	11,813	15,840	1,470
Next 155 giving turnover figures	4,641	8,769	673
Remaining Companies	11,448	(11,400)[1]	4,787
Total	27,900	(36,000)[1]	6,930

The fact is that the largest British firms have come to rely on the medium and smaller companies to supply the exports for the balance of payments. What has still to be made clear are the reasons for the giant companies continuing with their overseas investment although as we saw earlier the return to capital is no higher than at home. The explanation is bound up in the whole analysis of the role of the international company in modern capitalism. Given the nature of the capitalist world marker and the lines of production into which industrial investment is attracted inside that market, there was nothing else they could do. The reasons for the growth of the international company include control of raw materials, the planning of flows through all the stages of production, flexibility and spreading of risks among different plants, the detection of technical innovations at an early stage of research and development, above all the establishment of a large captive market for long runs of production, which only advertising on an international scale can guarantee. Including in this last point must be the claim to participate in world cartels and agreements for fixing prices and sharing markets.

---

1. The figures in brackets are a guess; total final output at home was about £37,000 million but this includes imports and taxes on expenditure and excludes sales abroad by British companies subsidiaries

Labour and the Crisis of the World Economy

As is becoming very evident, a major crisis is developing for the first time since the war in the whole world economy. Up to 1966 world production and world trade, at least in manufacturing, had grown at unprecedented rates – in the last eight years respectively averaging in volume 7% and 8% a year. In such circumstances it was not difficult even for a backward British industry to increase exports at an average 4% a year. By 1967 the main forces that had sustained this growth were becoming worked out. They may be rapidly listed.

There was first the recovery of the defeated nations and the increase in trade inside Wester Europe engendered by the transfer of manpower from agriculture to industry and the internal exchange of goods within the European Economic Community. By 1967 the transfer of manpower and the tariff cuts which had produced this result was complete. Secondly there has been the huge outflow of capital both public and private from the United States associated with a great increase in overseas military spending. Since the surplus of United States began from 1958 onwards to run a steady balance of payments deficit of around $3 billion a year. This was financed by sales of gold which reduced the stock of gold in Fort Knox by 1962 to the level it has been in 1920. Attempts were therefore made in 1962 by the US private company overseas earnings. But the war in Vietnam once more raised the level of US military spending overseas and several countries led by France began to convert their dollar reserves into gold.

A crisis of liquidity, as the reserves of the great trading nations are called, arose. Gold was still being produced at the rate of over $1 billion a year but the possibility of gold being revalued in terms of the dollar led to nearly all of the new production in the capitalist world being upset by private hording. For a time Soviet and Chinese sales of gold to pay for imports of grain kept the gold reserves rising. In 1966 they actually began to fall for the first time since the war. The deficits on Britain's balance of payments in 1963,1964,1965 and 1966 provided some increase in available sterling. More important, an increase in 1965 of $2 billion in the reserve quotas of the International Monetary Fund improved the situation for a time. The hard fact remained in 1967 that world liquidity, which had been the equivalent of the value of over seven months of world trade movements in 1958 was down to 1967 to the equivalent of only three months trading. Without new forms of credit, trade was being strangled. What was equally serious, the underdeveloped primary producing countries were equivalent in 1967 to less than three months of their trading and most of these reserves – the Sterling Area countries not at all – over their holdings in 1956.

Reserves of the less developed countries were equivalent in 1967 to less than three months of their trading and most of these reserves were held by just five comparatively small countries – Venezuela, Israel, Saudi Arabia, Malaysia and Thailand. But a third of Britain's trade is still with the Sterling Area countries and a half of that with the less developed ones, of which only Malaysia and Kuwait count any reserves.

A very real danger arose in 1966 when three greatest trading nations, the United States, Britain and West Germany, simultaneously began to pursue policies designed to reduce their own balance of payments deficits without putting anything in the place of the finance these deficits had provided for other countries trade. The danger of a succession of beggar-my-neighbour policies of the kind experienced in 1931. The danger this time was not of competitive tariff-raising; this is now precluded by the General Agreement on Tariff and Trade. There was still, and is still, a danger of beggar-my-neighbour deflationary policies, combined here and there with devaluation. If several large countries try to balance their payments by increasing their exports and reducing their imports through deflationary measures the net result is almost bound to be a general reduction in the trade of all of them and thus in the trade of all other countries. This is what happened in 1931 and it can happen again.

How far was realisation of this danger which Mr Wilson expressed at the T.U.C. Conference in 1965 the reason for the Labour Government's vacillating attempts between 1964 and 1967 to avoid either sharp inflation or devaluation? Were there no alternatives open to the Government when it came to power and was faced by a balance of payments deficit of some £800 million?

The Rake's Progress

Harold Wilson in opposition had always argued that Tory Stop-Go and all that it implied could be avoided by the use of physical controls – the steering wheel in place of the alternation of brake and accelerator. "Ruthless discrimination will be practiced" he promised in the spring of 1964 so that "growth should not be stopped when imports threatened to rise too fast... Essential industries will be encouraged, those of lower priority will be held back". The 1964 Labour Party Manifesto had proposed long term trade agreements with Commonwealth countries to build stability into our foreign trade. The 1966 Manifesto had argued for a "concerted world effort... to enable overseas countries to earn the foreign exchange essential for their developed programmes... international commodity agreements and arrangements for finance for increasing and stabilising the export earnings of primary producing countries".

Mr Wilson himself had spoken at the 1963 Labour Party Conference on "Labour and the Scientific Revolution" in the following terms:

> "The Stop-Go economy of the last 12 years failed because the expansionary phase had not created growth in those industries which could provide a permanent breakthrough in Britain's export trade or a lasting saving in imports... Monetary planning is not enough. What are needed are structural changes in British industry and we are not going to achieve those on the basis of pre-election spurts every four years in our industry, or of hope of selling the overspill of the affluent society in the highly developed markers of Western Europe. What we need are new industries and it will be the job of the next Government to see that we get them... When we set up new industries based on science there need be no argument about location, no costly bribes to private enterprise to go here rather than there. We shall provide the enterprise and we shall decide where is goes." (*The Times, 2-10-63).*

What happened? We had first Mr Wilson's commitment at a Mansion House banquet in the City of London that "Sterling would be kept riding high". Devaluation was ruled out but there was still the promised alternative to deflation and "Stop-Go" stagnation. By 1964 the size of the payments deficit would have required physical control on imports, on foreign exchange movements and on building and investment at home.

In large part the crisis in the balance of payments was due to heavy overseas military expenditure and a hue flow of capital in the months before Labour took office. But there were in turn related to the requirements of an international economic, political and military system which imposed constraints on Britain freedom to act. To deal with the problems of debt and deficit in any radical way would as we shall see have involved an immediate confrontation, not only with this international system but also with those elements of it – the British financial institutions and large firms – through which Labour intended to act in order to modernise the economy. The very institutions that would be forced to give up their private interests to the will of an elected government were the only institutions through which the economy could be managed unless socialist institutions were designed to replace them. And it was of course just this option of the creation of socialist institutions which the Labour leadership had given up in advance. What was intended as a compromise became first a constraint and finally a capitulation. The elected Government could direct and manage everyone and everything else, but not capital.

The immediate form of the payment crisis was an increasing imbalance between exports and imports particularly with respect to manufactured goods. In fact a system of international division of labour in the advance capitalist world means that the import of manufactured goods is always growing. On top of this it was clear that British industry was no longer fully competitive with the new industries on the continent of Europe and in Japan, and this ironically was due to a failure of investment because of the Stop-Go policies imposed as a reaction to the previous balance of payments crisis. Devaluation would have corrected the immediate competitive situation. But those on the Left who advocated devaluation did so as part of a package of proposals for direct physical intervention in the economy by the government.

In the event, the Government of 1964 neither devalued nor deflated. The import surcharge of 15% in 1964, reduced to 10% in 1965, and abolished in 1966, was no alternative to devaluation. It was designed to reduce imports but did nothing to expand imports. A small increase in interest rates, an attempt at income restraint, and a massive loan took the place of deflation until this was finally accepted in July 1966. Labour's commitments to increase pensions, remove health charges and expand school building and public sector housing were fulfilled. But no corresponding cuts were made in the private sector and among the rich. Thus, with fully utilised resources and only a very modest increase in productivity from investment in the last years of Tory rule, it was inevitable that imports would be pulled in again faster than exports could rise.

The deflationary measures of July 1966 were designed to cut back all spending by a credit squeeze and a stop on wages. But the Government was caught once more, as previous Tory Governments had been, but the fact that the very measures taken to deflate – increased interest rates and taxes on consumption – only served to raise prices. Moreover, reduced sales in the home market raised unit costs and checked the investment plans of firms trying to expand in export markets. It was clear that exports were failing to catch up with imports. The gap between them widened steadily in the last quarter of 1966 and the first half of 1967. This was before the Suez closure and the dock strikes.

The first mistake in Labour's policies lay in supposing that it is possible to increase efficiency with programmes which retard overall growth. The attempt to sustain investment in the regions of high unemployment while holding back growth elsewhere could never succeed. Firms that don't intend to increase their capacity anyway, because of the depressed market are not going to invest anywhere despite, are not going to invest anywhere despite the extra grants offered in the "black" regions. All that the grant does is to provide private industry with a gift of doing what it would have done anyway. And what it will not do is in effect not done by anyone.

The second and far more serious mistake was to suppose that it was possible to reconcile the needs of the low-paid and the pensioners with so-called incentives to management and private capital; the growth of the public sector with avoidance of cuts in the private sector; economic growth for raising living standards at home with the preservation of the pound as a world currency and the City of London as its custodian. To pursue any one set of policies realistically would have meant rejecting the other set. It was this fact of choice that was hidden by the idea of a political consensus in an undifferentiated "New Britain".

The facts intervened. In the Autumn of 1967 unemployment was already running at above 3% for men and at 2.4% overall. The public sector which had played a crucial part in the relatively expansive and progressive phase of British new capitalism, was being rapidly run down and out. In 1960 employment for men in coal, on the railways, in gas, water, and electricity undertakings and in the steel industry, amounted to 11+1/2% of all male employment. By 1964 this had been reduced to just over 10% and after three years of Labour government to less than 9%. By 1971 it will have fallen to 7+1/2% given current proposals for reducing the mining industry and rationalising steel. This melting away of the public sector meant a return to the old callous pre-war labour and manning policy in key sectors of the economy. The long losses of the wage freeze and of rising prices combines with these other factors to make it inevitable that the Government's policies for rationalism and "spare capacity" were resisted.

This resistance led to strikes in the docks and elsewhere which were of course very damaging to the economy and which provoked a new general crisis. But these strikes were not accidents, they were the inevitable result of the real economic policy being followed. Only policies which provided new jobs, less inequality and more control of the workers whose livelihood was threatened. In fact the Government was creating fewer jobs, more inequality and less union control over conditions of work. It is enough to point out that the major conflicts have been between the Government and the Unions, and not between the Government and the employers.

So the British Economy has not grown. Production was stagnant but imports were continuing to rise. No alternative trading agreements had been made with Communist and other trading partners, in the Commonwealth and elsewhere, who were planning their economies and could have entered planned trade agreements. Devaluation was finally forced upon the government.

The Effects of Devaluation

Devaluation by itself solves nothing: it provides the opportunity for a solution – or rather for different solutions of Britain's crisis. Combined with physical controls over the home market and over foreign exchange movements it could have been used by the Labour Government at any time from November 1964 onward to prepare the way for a socialist solution. Three years later it is being combined with deflation and cuts in Government spending in an attempt at a capitalist solution. Since devaluation means that the prices of our imports rise as well as the prices of our exports falling in terms of foreign currencies, it is evidently on the balance between the two effects that devaluation will bye judged by any person or by any company.

For most exporters a 15% devaluation means that costs can be expected to rise by only about 5% (or 7% including the loss of the exports rebate) so that they should be able to cut their foreign prices by up to 8%. Whether they will or will not depends on how much extra they can hope to sell by lowering the prices of their particular products. British exporters have had their prices squeezed in foreign markets recently and many have probable been making little to no profit on their exports. They may be expected to raise their profit margins now, but the 8% improvement in their competitive position only puts them back where they were in 1963. This is because since then productivity in West Germany for example has risen by just over 8% faster than it has in Britain. What is more, we have to face the fact that growth in the world market is slowing down and every increase in the sales of British firms must from now be on almost entirely at the expense of foreign firms.

Consensus politics were only possible in a viable British economy; a crisis of the world market would deliver the *coup de grace*. What then is the prospect, writing as we do at the end of 1967? If new plans are quickly put into operation for increasing world liquidity and world trade maintains its expansion, and if exactly the right balance is found between home and foreign demand for British industry to expand at minimum units costs, with minimal labour troubles, then exports would probably rise rapidly and a large surplus would be established on the balance of payments at least by 1969. A home-based boom could follow in 1970 in time for the next election. But even in these most favourable conditions, we should not forget that the result would be a very sharp change in the division of the national product between capital and labour. Profits would boom while real earnings would be held back by the rising price of imported foods. Higher food prices and cuts in government spending, predicated to allow for increased exports, would hit particularly hard at pensioners and lower income groups.

These most favourable assumptions, which are being widely made by the economists, are based on most uncertain foundations. The new plans for increased world liquidity are in abeyance until the US government reduces its payments deficit, a reduction which in itself will worsen the liquidity position. Gold might still be revalued if the deficit is not reduced.

Although this would increase world liquid reserves it would not help Britian, which has no gold, and the competitive revaluations that followed might leave Britain where she had been before November 1967. Even if nothing more serious happens in the next year or so the devaluation of the pound has greatly weakened the purchasing power of all the other Sterling Area countries. The value of their reserves is reduced, and they may have much more difficulty than the British industry in benefiting by extra sales for their primary products in world markets. This especially applies to less developed countries, which may have been important markets for British exports.

The assumption that the balance of home and foreign demand can be got just right is more doubtful even than the assumption about the growth of the world market. The reasons for having such doubts is that the only measures which the Government is allowing itself to use to reduce home demand, in order to make room for meeting new export orders, all cut into wages and into demand of the poor while leaving capital and the demand of the rich unscathed. These measures – of cutting government expenditure on the social services and of freezing wages – are the only weapons in the Governments armoury since it refuses to use discriminatory physical controls. We have already seen that income restraint was not at any point used to discriminate in favour of even the lower paid worker. If Mr. Jenkins now introduces what is called "selectivity" in the social services it will not be to give greater help to the poorest, but to cut the whole bill without the poorest suffering any *extra* loss. This has always been the objection of socialists to selectivity – rent rebate schemes, payment for prescriptions etc. – that it was an excuse for general cuts in public services and would inevitably lead to the reemergence of two services, one for the poor and one for the rich.

A continuing wage freeze and cuts in social services might just be tolerated a little longer, if production for export began at once to take up the slack. No one, however, believes that this will happen quickly. The cuts are to come first and the export-led expansion is to follow. Some increases in output at home may soon occur to replace higher costs imports, but the prospect of a high level of unemployment for many months seem assured. This is partly because of the rapid rundown that is planned for manpower in at least three industries – steel, coal and the railways. The last two of these are particularly labour intensive and located in regions where without special government intervention there will be no export industries or import substituting industries.

If unemployment at least in the "black" regions is added to frozen wages and social service cuts, then a major collision of Government and Labour is inevitable. If general employment can be held down then the Government might get by with a continuation only of the minor battles that have marked its progress since taking office. It could take on the miners and the steel workers separately as it has taken on defeated one by one the seamen, the dockers, the busmen, the railwaymen. It can hardly, hope, however, to avoid a still further straining of loyalties and still further spread on the mood of anger and the sense of betrayal that is now rife throughout the Labour Movement.

Conditions will not be propitious for co-operation between Unions, government and employers in the massive redeployment and retraining which modernisation and rationalisation imply. Whatever agreements unemployment is strong and Mr. Callaghan's threat of the need for a wider margin of resources is fulfilled. It is hard to believe that, without using the physical controls we have suggested, the Government could manage a deteriorating situation after devaluation in any other way than by the most ruthless capitalist measures. The Unions would have to be divided and their power broken. The Left would be finally alienated from the Government and the basis for a new coalition government would exist. What can still save the Labour Party as it now exists is only the revival of world trade and a series of lucky strokes (not strikes!) in getting the balance of home and foreign demand exactly right at every stage.

Conclusion on a Programme of Demands for the Labour Movement

It would be wholly unrealistic to suppose that the present Labour Government can be moved to change its policies in the immediate future. On the other hand, it would be fatal for the Left to retreat into local notions for local gains and for local groups of workers, without holding out an overall alternative programme to advance the understanding and confidence of the movement in its future. There is a special danger that local militancy inside certain Unions, and particularly those inside in advanced sectors of the economy, could very well be reconciled – as the Unions in the USA have become reconciled – with policies that are opposed to the interest of the majority of the people.

It would only be too easy for some sections of British Trade Unions to follow the American path, and to support industrial modernisation only to allow British capital to try and catch up with US capital at its own game, to improve the positions of workers in the more advanced sectors at the expense of the rest, to become even more tied to the emphasis on the production of private goods at the expense of public services. It is the danger of this division between different groups of workers in the more and the less advanced sectors of industry that makes the establishment of united action so essential. The demands which are put forward from the Left must always have the aim first of uniting the widest range of support from the ranks of Labour and secondly of being seen to make real cuts into the power of capital. No programme which does not include a tax on private wealth and a corresponding expansion of public investment, into industry as well as services, can hope to meet such requirements.

But an effective response from the whole Labour Movement would have to go further. It would need to be two-pronged – on the one hand demanding the extension of workers' control over the processes and costing of production and particularly over the sharing of work as automation reduces labour requirements and creates higher profits in the most advances industrial sectors; on the one hand, demanding that controls be placed upon private industry – partly physical controls that would be imposed as a condition of state assistance – control over prices for example and control over the investment of pension and insurance funds and the much more discriminating use of grans and loans to industry in relation to performance in research, expert markets, location, reduced hours of work for the same pay, educational and retraining provisions etc.

Finally, the very backwardness of British industry, especially in relation to the United States, demands a special response From Labour, if further American domination is to be avoided. On the one hand, wider trade associations would have to be established with other countries, not as in E.E.C. through supernational and exclusive agreements, but through specifically planned joint development projects to find wide enough markets to challenge American technological domination in certain fields; on the other hand, Labour's promised science-based industries under public control would have to be directed to meeting precisely those needs which US capitalism most neglects – the health services and low cost housing for example.

Above all in a period of rapidly increasing mechanisation the major task of Labour must be to bear witness to its historic claim that the object of production: should not be commodities but man, that is not the quantities of goods but the quality of life that matters, and particularly in the human relationships at work which must still occupy the greater part of men's lives.

Michael Barratt-Brown

OPENING THE BOOKS

The Institute for Workers' Control

Pamphlet Series No. 4   One shilling and sixpence

WORKERS' CONTROL —
Opening the books

Introduction

The demand for opening the books has become a central demand of the movement for Workers' Control. The notes attached to this introduction suggest some of the questions that workers' control groups would want to find answers to as they began in fact to open the management's books. Every governing class in history has tried to clothe the business of government in mystery, and the clerks who carried on the actual business have always resorted to magic words and signs to blind the ignorant. It is not for nothing that the most representative organisation of British business-men and financiers is the secret society of Freemasons. There are indeed some real secrets in business — the technical know-how and experience of firms (not of course patents, which by their very name imply that they are open but protected by law from theft). Most of the secrets, however, have nothing to do with competition but everything to do with confusing the uninformed worker. They are useful not only for concealing profits but also for concealing managerial efficiency. This should not be taken to imply that secrets relating to competition are permissible. Secrecy about plans for a new product may lead to wasteful investment elsewhere.

In fact a great deal of information is now available in the annual company accounts of firms with a quotation on the Stock Exchange. Private companies are still permitted to conceal most of their accounts. Many firms make the Company Accounts available to their employees and summaries of the accounts of all quoted firms are available from Moodies Services and the Stock Exchange Yearbook (see References at end of notes). The first necessity for groups of workers who wish to master the secrets of their firms is to learn to master the intricacies of Company Accounts. The Labour Research Department's little handbook on *How to Read a Balance Sheet* provides a good introduction and other books that go into greater detail will be found in the Reference at the end of the Notes. The Labour Research Department to which many Trades Councils and Unions are affiliated will also look up on request what other information is available in Bush House where the company registers are kept. In this way workers' control groups can find details of shareholdings in their company.

It must be made clear that "Opening the Books" is not just a matter of reading hitherto concealed facts and figures. It is a starting point, but no more than a starting point, to *evaluating* and *interpreting* a complex situation in order to work out and fight for a policy of advance towards democratic control of industry. Even when the books are opened they will not be opened wide. a good many facts will be held back and there will also be facts that are needed but not known. It would be wrong to hold back the shaping of policies and aims awaiting fuller facts. On the contrary policies based on the best available facts should be used to focus attention on the need for better information. The charge of authority against critics who have not access to the facts must be turned into a boomerang. Industrial democracy, workers' control over measures to raise productivity, improved conditions etc., imply a generally available, first-rate information system.

After the Accounts and other published information of the Company have been mastered, three quite different types of questions will require answers;

(a) Questions about the true financial position of the company that may be concealed by the accounts;
(b) Questions about the techniques of management used by company's and the result of these techniques in company structure;
(c) Questions about the social costs and benefits of the company's activities.

The questions listed in the Notes are organised under six headings —

A The Product and Productive Processes
B Organisation and Management
C Sales and Marketing
D Finance and Pricing
E Employment Policy
F Contribution to the Community

Inevitably, however, certain questions come under several headings and there are managerial, financial and social questions to ask under each heading. A word is perhaps required here about each of these types of questions.

Managerial techniques are becoming increasingly sophisticated and University and Technical College courses are now devoted to them. An excellent introduction is the B.B.C. Publication *Fothergale Co. Ltd.*, (see References at end). Some of these techniques will seem pretty complicated at first sight and Workers' Control Groups will need to take advantage of Day Release Courses and Technical College courses if they are to master them.

Technical Colleges etc., have many excellent people teaching management science—and some not so excellent—but the content of what is taught nonetheless needs to be looked at critically. Management science did not grow up with industrial democracy in mind. As the requirements of workers' control groups develop new approaches and new types of classes will have to be introduced into the teaching of management. From this in turn it follows that a great deal more public funds will need to be spent on research into management techniques, use of computers, economic evaluation etc., by people who see things from the point of view of industrial democracy, working on problems raised by people who are trying to introduce new forms of industrial democracy. Groups need to be aware in their thinking and style of work from the outset that they must fight for research and educational backing of a new type to help and support their work and to be controlled by people who see the problems in the way that those who are trying to apply industrial democracy in practice see them.

There is no possibility nor need for members of control groups to master all the intricacies of modern magagement techniques. On the other hand these must not be left as mysteries on which the expert even in the groups says the last word "take it or leave it". Different people in the group, according to interest and experience, can specialise on particular aspects of economics and management which they will come to understand better than others in the team. In this way it should be possible for all members of the team to understand the main issues and principles underlying particular problems. The future of good organisation lies with team-work as against heirarchical authority. (Policy shaping by teams does not conflict with assigning individual executive responsibility. Control teams could well be the embryo of new administrative structures.)

Most of the techniques of management are in fact fairly simple but they tend to be described for brevity's sake in the mathematical and statistical shorthand terms that economists use. Financial and Pricing Policy is of course a part of management technique but it has important connections with government policy and other wider economic considerations. It should be made clear here that industry, in Britain at least, is exceedingly backward in its techniques of investment decision making. To take an example, if workers do not understand what "discounted cash flow" means, they can reassure themselves by realising that most managements do not understand this either. Very briefly it is a way of measuring the profitability of different investment projects. The measurement is made by calculating the present value of a sum to be received in the future, taking into account the number of years and the compound rate of interest.

Questions about Social Costs and benefits are mentioned under many different headings. These are the costs and benefits to society which are not taken into consideration in the firm's accounts. An important question in Cost-Benefit analysis is who pays the cost and who benefits. This is already being studied in relation to government taxes and expenditures, but the application of such analysis to company policies has hardly been developed at all. This is because the assumption of a free market economy is that the choice of the consumer in the market combined with the price mechanism in the market will allocate resources in the best possible way for society. When firms can fix prices and use advertising to persuade consumers to buy what they produce, the assumptions of the free market have to be questioned. They have always been open to question on another ground, that the free market economy may leave resources of manpower and equipment unemployed and thus fail to assure the optimum resource allocation.

It will be clear from the emphasis on the social implications of Company policy that something wider is being proposed here than an improved bargain between workers and management in industry. What is being proposed is the establishment of Workers' Control Groups that would act as social audit groups for their particular factories. The reasoning behind such a proposal is that without bringing in such wider social questions workers' control groups attempting to extend their power will very soon come up against the rigid framework of existing social and economic policies within which firms operate. The corrollary of an extension of workers' control into social audit is that individual workers' control groups will need both a centre for exchanging information and a wider political arm for challenging the existing framework. A chain of workers' control groups in many different firms and industries throughout the Country could begin to afford to finance a Research and Information Exchange Centre. From this it would be a natural extension to set up National Social Audit Groups, consisting of engineers, scientists, accountants and workers' representatives which could bring pressure to bear on Parliament and Government. One of the most natural demands would be an extension of the powers of the Select Committee on Nationalised Industries and the establishment of a Select Committee on Private Industry to report on the use of public funds (now running at something over £1,000 millions a year) in grants and loans to private industry. An obvious example is the crying need for a national audit to examine the costing assumptions of the Government's Fuel Policy and a social audit unit to examine the implications of pit c'osures for the economy of whole areas which are now dependent on the coal industry for employment.

The questions that follow under headings (A) to (F) should be regarded as a "check list", that is a list that organisers of a group would work through to select particular issues around which to start work. The scope of these questions is very large and a very limited selection must be taken as a starting point. There will be many questions not included in this list. Each group's work will be a "criticism in practice" of the list out of which suggestions and new experience will flow which can be made available to other groups.

Michael Barratt-Brown
Sheffield, March 1968

A PRODUCTION

1. *The Product or Product Mix —*
   a) What is it for? What priority for society as a whole? Who is it for? What priority for individuals?
   b) Could it be made better for its purpose, safer, cheaper? Would it be worth making better, cheaper, safer — from individual or social view point.
   Test by estimated social costs as well as market price.
   c) Has the Consumer Association tested it? Or were other independent performance tests made? What was the firm's response to the tests if unfavourable?
   d) Is there much waste in production? What use is made of by-products? Would it be worth reducing waste? — once again test by private and social cost.
   e) Is demand likely to continue for product as incomes rise, tastes change, technology changes?
   Could a cheaper model widen the market?
   f) What alternative lines are being researched, developed for the future — once again what for and who for?

2. *Research and Development —*
   a) What is the firm's policy?
   b) How much spent —on pure research
   — as % of turnover
   — on different types
   of research, including packaging.
   c) What use of other research facilities, contacts with other firms? On what terms are these shared?
   d) How do they compare with similar firms?
   e) Query delays or failure to adopt new ideas — reasons?
   f) Does firm rely on foreign company patents or know-how?

3. *Machinery used in Production —* distinguish the different processes.
   a) Is it the best for the job in each process? Would it

be worth improving it? — social and private cost of doing so or not doing so.
d) Is it bought on open tender, from associated company,
c) Is it safe?
d) It is bought on open tender, from associated company, 'friends' or hired?
e) Is it well arranged for transfer between machines?
f) Would transfer machines be worth using?
g) Is method study used? If so by whom and for what purpose?
h) How much sub-contracting? On what terms?

Transport and Transfer — distingish departments, plants, firms.
a) How much unecessary travelling?
b) Is any of the system unsafe or wasteful?
c) Would a new lay out be worthwhile? How test production flow? Is critical path analysis used?
d) Is the equipment adequate — locos, cranes, belts, fork lifts, trolleys etc.
e) Are internal roads and rails properly kept, designed, safe?
f) Are social costs considered in use of road or rail or other transport?
g) What determined location of plants — note social and private costs.

Purchasing and Stocks — distinguish departments and plants
a) Are stocks adequate, too large — note individual and social cost of holding inadequate or excessive stocks.
b) How are materials purchased — from own organisation, wholesalers, bulk orders?
c) What programming system is used?
d) Are stocks well placed, controlled, recorded. (See Finance).
e) Is there much Work in Progress — as % of Turnover?
f) Is there long delay waiting for parts?
g) Could co-operation be developed with other firms?
h) Is liaison between departments good?

Quality Control —
a) What system of sampling and testing at different stages? Would it be worth improving?
b) How is batch size determined?

c) Are there too many models, varieties? Would standardisation make the consumer suffer?
   d) Is quality regularly altered rather than price?

ORGANISATION AND MANAGEMENT
1. *Directors and Leading Executives*
   a) Who are they? How many from founding family, from outside banking and finance, from inside management? How many relatives? How many full-time, part-time?
   b) What are their qualifications? How many Scientists, Technologists? What other directorships?
   c) What are they paid?
      What other emoluments do they receive — car, chauffeur, petrol allowance, private secretary, subsidised meals, free life insurance, insurance for private medical treatment, pension provision, covenants for private schooling of children, subsidised housing, bonus payments, any other extras?
   d) Are they connected with any political party or industrial pressure group?
      Active in employers' associations.
   e) What is the dismissal procedure for them? How much notice? 'Golden hand shake'?

2. *Management Structure* — distinguish staff and line command
   a) How are top decisions made, co-ordinated?
   b) What is the span of responsibility?
   c) How much real delegation — firm, plant, department?
   d) How much long-term planning?
   e) Is a computer used?

3. *Proportions of Manpower in different sectors:*
   a) Staff: R. & D., design and testing, finance and accounts, sales and publicity.
   b) Line: Lower management and supervisors.
   c) Production processes including packing.
   d) Maintenance and Repair.
   e) Transport
      Are any excessive? How could you test this?

4. *Consultation* — i.e. Ideas going upwards as well as downwards.
   a) What provision for Workers' Council, Workers' Representation at different levels?
   b) How are these men chosen? Elected? Nominated?

c) What proportion of workers' representation to management?
d) What power do Councils have?
   Who takes the chair? Are minutes kept?
e) What specialist committees on production, maintenance, safety, training, etc.?
f) What provision for shop stewards meeting time and space at company expense?
g) Is management based on hierarchy of orders or process of committee consultation at all levels? Can you compare with other firms?

Records and Statistics — by firm, Plant, Department
a) What system? Who's responsible? At each level? Is a computer in use?
b) What check on decisions made at each level?
c) How much collaboration with government — Board of Trade, Ministry of Labour?
d) Are returns, honest, accurate?
e) Are records flexible i.e. usuable for other purposes than those for which collected.

Use of Computers
a) For what purposes are computers used?
   1. In production control?
   2. To replace clerical work?
   3. For technical and scientific calculations?
   4. For accountancy?
   5. What other uses are made of the computer?
b) Is there an integrated management information system? Or plans to introduce one? Is there a data-banking system to hold available information on production? To whom is information available?
c) How is data collected and put in computer-reading form?
d) Does your organisation own its own computer? Will it use the G.P.O. computer utility? Should it have a policy in relation to the G.P.O. utility?
e) Are computer codes used for transmitting information outside of the firm?
f) Have effects of introducing computers been good or bad for employees? What form do consultations about the effects of introducing computers take? About the purposes for which computers should be used? About production policy in relation to computers?

7. *Recruitment and Training*
   a) Management — family, internal, ladder external advertising.
   b) Training at all levels — internal or external (and see E.7 below).
   c) Promotion systems and other incentives.
   d) Opportunities to cross 'class' barriers?
   e) What manpower budgeting is made?
8. *Sub-Contracting* — firm's policy
   a) How much?
   b) On what basis?
   c) How controlled?
   d) Attitude of sub-contractors to Trade Unions?
   e) What tests to apply for using sub-contractors?
9. *Stock Control* — see above A5
10. *Capacity Working* —
    a) Who decides on capacity? How is the decision reached?
    b) What control on unit costs (See below D.6.)

C **SALES AND MARKETING** (See Also D.7)
1. Company Policy concerning growth — Sales record over the last decade by shares.
   a) Home market sales
   b) Exports
   c) Overseas subsidiaries sales. How are markets estimated?
2. Method of sales — wholesalers, agents. retailers, own outlets.
       — how to improve?
3. Margins added to ex-factory price. Could they be reduced?
4. Cost of packaging and advertising relative to production.
       — Could they be reduced? How tested?
5. Relations between sales and production departments
       — re quality control, new models, servicing.
6. Possibility of bulk orders for long runs in home market or export market — co-operation with government.
7. Differential pricing and discounts for special customers.
       — How controlled? How tested?

D **FINANCE**
1. Description of Company — Private, Public, Holding,

Subsidiary.
2. Sources of Finance —**Equity or Family**
 — Preference Capital
 — Loans
 — Mortgages
 — Bank Overdrafts
 — In what proportion? What is cost of total finance per cent?
 — Could it be reduced? How compare with other firms?

3. Profits — record over past decade — profit per employee, profit per sales turnover
 — if a private company is balance sheet published?
 — if not, why not?

4. Dividend Payments and Reserves
 — What is company policy — on dividends, capital capital issues?

5. Major Financial Decisions.
 — Who makes them? — External or internal directors?
 — How do schemes get considered?
 — Who has initiative?

6. Criteria for Investment Decisions
  a) How is plant depreciated?
     How are assets valued?
  b) Is old plant considered in relation to new schemes?
  c) What system for evaluating return to capital? — pay-out period, Book rate, Average Ratio, Discounted Cash Flow?
  d) On what rate of return are schemes acceptable?
  e) What are outside considerations?
     — family, other shareholders, institutions, take-over threats.

7. Pricing Policy —
  a) cartel membership
  b) gentlemens' agreements
  c) 'price leadership'
  d) 'cost plus'
  e) price competition — of what sort?

8. Cost Calculation — How made to include:
  a) sharing of overheads
  b) cross subsidising between departments

       c) allowance for by-products
       d) capital replacement
       e) stock
       f) social costs
       g) government allowances
         — Is marginal costing used and how is forecasting done?
9. Assets — How are these valued? How often reviewed? — Any evidence of undervaluing?

E EMPLOYMENT POLICY

1. Structure of Earnings (and fringe benefits)
      — managerial
      — other technical and administrative
      — clerical — male and female
      — supervisory — male and female
      — manual — male and female — skilled
                                    — unskilled
                                    — semi-skilled
  — What is policy regarding structure?
  — What is the dispersion of earnings? Too great? How reduce?
  — What anomalies? How test?
  — Are earnings at any level linked to profitability? If so what criteria?

2. Wage and Salary Negotiation.
  — How is this done by different Unions?
    a) national — on what criteria — productivity, cost of living
    b) local — piece rates — how set? Measured Day Work, What Norms? Output bonuses— department or plant
    c) personal — which workers not organised? Why?
  — How to achieve greater unity among workers — wage and salary?

3. Hiring and Firing
    a) What consultation if any? How to improve?
    b) What notice? What safeguards?
    c) Closed Shop?
    d) What joint examination of wage and salary earners at redundancy and in reorganisation?
    e) What transfer schemes to other parts of organisation?
    f) How to improve position of workers?
    g) Any queries about redundancy payments?

4. Manning of Machines
   a) Who decides on manning?
      Manual and Staff?
   b) What consultation — how far in advance?
   c) How improve workers' control?
5. Hours and Holidays — Distinguished different grades and departments.
   a) What hours averaged in fact?
      What holidays?
   b) How much overtime? Could it be reduced without loss of earnings?
   c) What shifts? How inconvenient?
   d) Work sharing in short-time. How possible?
6. Health and Safety
   a) What records are kept?
   b) Is there a factory doctor?
   c) Joint Safety Committees?
      Workmens inspectors?
   d) What check up system?
   e) What sports and social facilities?
   f) How improve? How compare with other firms?
   g) Company attitude to time off for sport, conferences, political work etc.?
7. Education and Training —
   a) What schemes for new entrants including apprentices?
   b) How much release? How much general education?
   c) What schemes for retraining?
      inside firm, in local colleges.
   d) What shop steward training and general adult education on release?
   e) What contribution to Training Fund? How much drawn from it?
8. Redundancy and Superannuation —
   a) What schemes apart from Redundancy Fund?
   b) How improve schemes?
   c) What control over redundancy by Unions?
   d) What policy for employing older men, disabled men on lighter work?

CONTRIBUTION TO THE COMMUNITY

1. National Government — Taxes, general co-operation with government policies.

The Bulletin of the Institute for Workers' Control
contributors include Michael Barratt-Brown, Stephen Bodington, Ken Coates, Royden Harrison, John Hughes, Bill Jones, Walter Kendall, Ian Mikardo, M.P., Ernie Roberts, Alan Rooney, Hugh Scanlon, Tony Topham and many others.

Quarterly, 96 pp. Single issues 8/-, Annual Subscription 30/- from 91 Goldsmith Street, Nottingham.

Pamphlet No. 2 of the Institute

is

Workers' Control and Productivity Bargaining

by

Tony Topham

Price 2/-

Bulk supplies of 250 copies or more of this pamphlet, and others of the Institute are available at cost price, for cash in advance £7-0-0.

Ken Coates and Tony Topham

THE LABOUR PARTY'S PLANS FOR INDUSTRIAL DEMOCRACY

The Institute for Workers' Control

Pamphlet Series No. 5

The Labour Party's Plans for Industrial Democracy

by Ken Coates and Tony Topham

It was symptomatic of the increasingly recognised importance of the issue that, after publishing one extended pamphlet on Industrial Democracy for the benefit of its youth movement (1) at the beginning of 1967, the National Executive Committee of the Labour Party returned to the same theme with a second major declaration (2), in June last year. At many points this second document contradicts its fore-runner, and in general it is a much more solid and better-thought-out affair.

Part of the reason for this is that the June statement is the report of a serious study-group, which included a number of highly competent participants, such as Jack Jones, the Assistant Executive Secretary of the Transport & General Workers' Union, John Hughes, Bill Simpson of the Foundryworkers' Union and Professor K. W. Wedderburn, together with several other industrial relations experts. Their report was unanimous, and it was introduced by the General Secretary of the Party, Mr. A. L. Williams, with these words:

> "A thorough discussion on this report might lead to far-reaching changes being made in the foundations of our industrial society, that will endure for a very long time."

So far, however, the discussion within the Labour Party itself has not developed very far, although it has certainly burgeoned in the independent socialist press, in the unions, and in the universities. This can hardly be an accident: careful examination of this report will raise the most profound questions about the desirability of the course of Governmental policy towards the trade union movement, and, indeed, at many points, the Labour Party statement runs exactly counter to the drift of present Government intervention in industrial relations.

The great merit of the report is that it registers, formally, within the official councils of the Labour Movement, the debate which has been raging, unofficially, on its margins for the past four or five years. All the many shortcomings of the document should be viewed in this light: that it places on the agenda, in a central

1. Industrial Democracy: A discussion document for the Young Socialists. The Labour Party, 1967 — Ninepence.
2. Industrial Democracy: Working Party Report. The Labour Party, 1967 — Two Shillings.

position, issues which have for too long been simply ignored or ducked. Once the branch rooms of the trade unions, and the factory committees of shop stewards, begin to consider this statement, they will quickly sharpen out their own ideas, which may well go far beyond the tentative explorations which have been made by the team.

For this reason the report must be welcomed, because it signals the end of the paralysing pseudo-politics which have produced the present Government, and which were based on a virtual conspiracy to avoid all the major issues of power, and fudge all the basic conflicts, which beset modern society. Before one can get the right answers, one must ask the right questions; and at last a significant body of trade union opinion has begun to do just this. It may take time to distil the solutions, but once this argument has opened up, it will take more than cunning and equivocation, those two staple responses of postwar British politics, to close it down again.

The Report should be discussed in this spirit.

For all that, the Report is marked by some serious handicaps. The most serious of all is that it approaches the whole given establishment of the State and its organs with considerable naivete. For a century and more, the State has been anything but neutral in the tug-of-war between capital and labour. It has intervened in every major upsurge of industrial unrest, in the face of every significant push towards industrial democracy, to head off and hold back the forces which might limit or control the powers of capital.

Today, the concentration of industrial power, and the pressure of international competition, have produced forcible tendencies to corporate forms of business organisation, and these in turn have gripped the State, which is clearly vulnerable, at every point, to the pervasive influence of the extended web of elite financial and managerial power. The new, increasingly corporate capitalism has abandoned much of the old entrepreneurial rhetoric about "risk" and "competition", and speaks with growing fervour of the need to "plan". So when the Labour Party Report speaks of the increasing acceptance of "the concept of purposive planning", it becomes necessary to ask the question "purposive for *whom?*" And *who* accepted it? The extension of indicative planning has nothing whatever to do with the democratic control of economic priorities, as has been clearly established in every major capitalist country in the past few years.

Even if one takes the nationalised sector of British economy, the Report grossly over estimates the degree of truly social, as opposed to commercial, independence available to "public" enterprise. It says:

> "there is less conflict felt as to the 'ends' of economic and social purposes of the firms and institutions concerned: some concept of 'public service' may create fewer barriers to the positive co-operation of work groups and their representatives than does that of profit-making for the owners of property".

This could be true if the public sector were growing and the private sector were rapidly shrinking: then the two concepts would be juxtaposed and their logic would be plain to all. But today the public sector is, in vital respects, shrinking: fuel and power, once mainly under public control, are, with pit closures and the development of North Sea Gas by private oil companies, suffering creeping but remorseless denationalisation: and in the process, the intensification of purely commercial competition in the declining public sector works in exactly the opposite way to that desired by the authors of the Report. Indeed, one of them, John Hughes, recognised the forces at work when he wrote of the exploitation of the public by the private sector, coining, some years ago, the graphic phrase 'business-mens' syndicalism' to describe this very process.

There are two moments in nationalisation which are of great significance if its meaning is to be grasped: first, as Meade has shown, in his book *Efficiency, Equality and the Ownership of Property* private property ownership was actually *augmented* by the extension of nationalisation, which has had the effect of increasing public debt and creating newly-liberated sources of interest-bearing wealth; but second, workers in nationalised industries are apt to be more politically conscious than others, which remains a key reason for advocating nationalisation. However, if it is true that coalminers learned, in the struggle against the coalowners, important lessons which were reinforced on vesting day, it is no less true that after vesting day their situation remained as conflict-ridden as ever. It would be wrong to try to persuade workers in the public sector that they might lower their guard in the interests of industrial co-operation. The miners have belatedly found this out. In the public, no less than the private sector, it is crucially important for the unions to build independent democratic controls, asserting their powers *against* management, at least until the economy at large can determine overall decisions on democratic criteria.

The Report makes a number of useful suggestions as to how legislation might strengthen industrial democracy. But it is far too circumspect to evaluate the results of the *actual* legislation, in which the Government is hecticly engaged, the great majority of which is working exactly contrary to the spirit which the Report wishes to foster. So, nothing is said about the restoration of the right to strike to its full amplitude, now badly weakened by the Prices and Incomes Act, and, if report is to be believed, about to be still further undermined by even more regressive legislation. Neither is anything said about the maintenance of a level of managed unemployment, unprecedented in the postwar period, whose first function is to increase 'disciplinary' pressure on the unions, or, in other words, to curtail and roll back those encroachments which many shop stewards have been able to make on managerial prerogatives. It is increasingly apparent to trade unionists that, rather than look towards the intervention of the Government to extend their powers on the shopfloor, they need to oil their weapons for use against that Government, as it bears down upon them with more and more officious restrictions of their most elementary rights.

Yet one looks in vain in the Report for an appropriate warning that the way to industrial democracy must be through a basic challenge to current Government strategies — through struggle and *necessary* militancy. Instead, the Report implies that the State's role is evolving in ways conducive to the advance of industrial democracy.

Having thrown vigilance to the winds in its approach to the State, the Report is ambiguous in its approach to the question of the *forms* of industrial democracy. The principal emphasis is on the need to extend workers' participation through the development of trade union bargaining rights — the principle of the "single channel of representation". It records its approval of the TUC's evidence to the Royal Commission, which stated that trade unions had in the past been too rigid in insisting that trade union independence required that they take no part in management.

The cry of trade union independence has often, wrongly, been used against the advocates of workers' control, with which it is of course perfectly compatible. But to suggest that trade union independence can safely take care of itself, whilst forms of participation are pursued by the unions, is to tread on dangerous ground. Genuinely independent workers' control requires *either* the advance, through encroachment, of independent shop floor powers won by struggle, *or* the building of committees which supervise and stand over and against the powers of management.

For this latter purpose, elected councils — or elected representatives — will be required. The trade unions should certainly be responsible for the elections of such councils or representatives. But there is nothing impracticable or unreal in the idea that workers should elect two sets of representatives to carry out two different functions — the traditional defensive role of the trade union bargaining machine, and the new offensive forms of workers' control over management.

The short truth is that the working party's advice stems from a desire to make practical recommendations about how *things should be changed* to extend industrial democracy. But the real problem is that of how *people* should be *stimulated* to demand such an extension. The purpose of any proposals for reform will be overborne by the established power-structure, without any real trouble, if this lesson is not learnt. This is the gross default of Mr. Wilson, who, before he attained office, spoke as if he were concerned to mobilise the initiative of all the workpeople as an explosive creative force; and after his preferment showed himself to be content to play the same kind of manipulative role as was enacted by his fore-runners.

There is one key area in which the Report makes suggestions for this kind of structural reform. This consists of its specific proposals for accountability, for the provision of basic information to workpeople, as a matter of right. The Report lists four headings under which companies should be compelled to provide full information to their employees.

These are so important that it is worthwhile to list them in full, with the arguments which are advanced to support the provision of such information. The Report says:

> "Just as the state, if it is to extend effective social accountability and make a reality of 'forward planning', must have access to more adequate information from companies, so must the trade unions if they are to protect their members' interests *and participate on equal terms in the direction of development.* We consider that the union or unions organising the labour force in a company should be ensured access to the information they require for effective bargaining and participation. Despite the recent strengthening of the requirements for disclosure of information contained in the new Companies Bill, we think that disclosure to bona fide trade unions has to be taken further (particularly so far as information on particular plants is concerned). The headings of importance, so far as disclosure to the trade unions is concerned, include:
>
> (i) *Manpower and Remuneration Questions*
> Labour force; labour turnover; manpower plan and staff development; absenteeism and sickness rates; accident rates and trends; accident prevention plans including training; other training schemes, labour costs per unit of output; payroll details and methods of payment; managerial and directorial emoluments; and qualifications of directors and senior manage-

ment. (An employer should, for instance, be obliged to tell his workers of any agreements made with other employers not to employ each others' recent employees.)

(ii) *Control Questions*
Details concerning holding, subsidiary, and associated companies; directors' shareholdings in the company; beneficial control of nominee shareholdings; internal management structure and definition of decision-making responsibilities.

(iii) *Development, Production and Investment Questions*
Proposed changes of a substantial character in methods of work and/or labour requirements; state of the order book and trend of orders gained and lost; research, development and investment plans; purchasing policies.

(iv) *Cost, Pricing and Profit Questions*
Cost and pricing structures; breakdown by plant or product applicable; turnover; financing of development.

It is important to consider how this information should be given. Just as the companies report annually to their shareholders, so they might be required to make annual reports to their workers which broadly covered this subject matter in general terms and was intelligently presented. But in addition unions should have the right of access to more detailed information under these headings, and on a continuing basis. Provision might have to be required for a limited right to withhold information, but only where it could be shown that publication, or transmission of information to a union, might involve a serious risk of harm to the firm's commercial interests".

The list covers important matters, and it should be discussed in detail. The object of trade unionists should be to extend it to make its teeth as sharp as possible: in this connection it will be noticed that two vital items which are missing are depreciation claims and the general question of reserves. Of course, these could, on a liberal interpretation, be subsumed under the heading of 'financing of development', although it would be wise not to assume that anyone will want to read such a declaration with undue liberalism, except, of course, the workpeople's representatives.

For some years now we have argued that it flies in the face of reason for any union to acquiesce in an incomes policy until *after* it has gained powers like those: for the very plain reason that the workpeople can not otherwise know whether they are being cheated until they have at least as much information about rentier incomes as the employers have about employee incomes. It would be a giant step forward if, having studied and developed the demands of this Report, the TUC would officially kill the incomes policy, and refuse to entertain any discussion at all about a new one until the return of full employment and the implementation of this measure of accountability. In the meantime, shop stewards and local bargainers could usefully press their employers to be as forthcoming with 'business secrets' as the Labour Party Report suggests.

But of course, these demands go right to the heart of our problem. Knowledge is power, and the power of capital is stored, not simply in the institutions of force which uphold the laws of Property, but firstly and most immediately, precisely in the secrecy of its accounts. This is plainly understood by the Prices and Incomes Board, which defends that power in the most naked and ingenuous terms, in its report on Productivity Bargaining:

> "There is the further question of how much information should be presented to trade unions. Clearly undertakings must be prepared to release more information than is normal in conventional negotiations if they are to win the confidence of the unions for this novel type of agreement and if they are to reach a successful settlement. We do not suggest, however, that all relevant information should be made available to trade union representatives, or indeed that the latter would necessarily wish this. Such facts might give the unions precise information on what the employer could pay before he had any notion of the figure for which they were prepared to settle. To decide whether and when to release this information is part of the art of negotiation, and unions as well as companies have their own differing stlyes of negotiation. One union officer will prefer to learn all he can about an undertaking's affairs, even if it means hearing a good deal of information which he must respect as confidential. He will see this as his best chance of serving the long-run interests of his members. Another will conceive it to be his duty to turn all he learns directly to their advantage in negotiations. To lay down instructions for all companies on how to negotiate productivity agreements with the unions, regardless of the methods preferred by the unions with which they deal, would be to ignore the facts of industrial relations."
>
> (PIB Report No. 36, pp 33-4)

On this matter, the voice of Mr. Aubrey Jones speaks authentically for what we can expect from the present Government, while the Report on Industrial Democracy is asserting the original aspirations of the trade unions. On a wider field, these are shaping up for a drastic and bitter collision.

If the battle for workers' control does not form up at the very centre of the unions' strategy during that collision, it will be a bleak day for labour, and, almost certainly, a bleak day for democracy. The present lethargic drift of the British Economy will not continue indefinitely. Either Labour will conscript capital, and in the process of a democratic upsurge, unleash the vast creative initiative of the British working people to re-organise the whole structure on a human basis, or, failing that, capital will decide that political democracy itself is an impediment to the rationalisation of its whole rickety edifice. Parliament is not eternal. Our strong man is lurking, somewhere, waiting for Mr. Wilson and Mr. Heath to conclude their pantomine. If he is to be held off and defeated, we must quickly awaken to the fact that democracy is a permanent self-deepening process, and that unless it is able to expand, it will die.

If only the Labour Movement can awaken to this challenge in time, if only the unions, from top to bottom, can elaborate their new demands in a dynamic, aggressive spirit, then there is time. We may not have long to say that.

PUBLICATIONS OF THE
INSTITUTE FOR WORKERS' CONTROL

PAMPHLET SERIES

1. The Way Forward for Workers' Control   Hugh Scanlon   1/6
2. Productivity Bargaining   Tony Topham   1/6
3. Labour and Sterling   M. Barratt-Brown   1/6
4. Opening the Books   M. Barratt-Brown   1/6
5. The Labour Party's Plan for Industrial Democracy   Ken Coates & Tony Topham   1/6

Bulk supplies of 250 copies or more of this pamphlet, and others of the Institute are available at cost price, for cash in advance £7-0-0.

ARCHIVE SERIES

1. Student Power   Bertrand Russell 6d.
2. Workers' Control & Revolution   Antonio Gramsci 1/-

The Bulletin of the Institute for Workers' Control

contributors include Michael Barratt-Brown, Stephen Bodington, Ken Coates, Royden Harrison, John Hughes, Bill Jones, Walter Kendall, Ian Mikardo, M.P., Ernie Roberts, Alan Rooney, Hugh Scanlon, Tony Topham and many others.

Quarterly, 96 pp.   Single issues 8/-, Annual Subscription 30/- from 91 Goldsmith Street, Nottingham.

Bob Harrison and Walter Kendall

workers' control and the motor industry

The Institute for Workers' Control

Pamphlet series No. 6   1/6d

THE RELEVANCE OF WORKERS' CONTROL TO THE STATE OF THE MOTOR INDUSTRY

A paper submitted by Bob Harrison.

It would be foolish to claim that any conscious, coherent demand for Workers' Control is coming from the car workers or the Unions which represent them. But there are massive and momentous changes taking place in the organisation of the industry and in the pattern of behaviour of the men and women employed therein. Their reaction to the control or management they experience at the point of production is probably the strongest evidence of the growing need for a new system of management. The present pattern of increasing resistance on the shop floor to the arbitrary decisions of management, is a reflection of the changing structure of the industry and the aggravation of the alienation symptoms experienced by the workers.

Economic forces will enforce continuing change in the structure and organisation of the industry and its relationship to the rest of the economy. Continuing change in the system of control inside the industry is likewise inevitable. It therefore must surely be the intent of both Trade Unionists and Socialists to channel the present workers' activity and organisation into positive demands for a new system of management, one responsible to those who do the work, and not to those who own the capital.

In action, Trade Unionists demand from their employment an increasing share of the income of the firm; improving working conditions (there is no absolute limit at which we will be content to let the matter rest), job-security and job satisfaction. We are at a stage of technological development in which it is possible for these aims to be satisfactorily progressed. They are complementary—and their satisfaction will require changes in ownership, control and management of industry. For the workers involved, their ability to create better jobs, and better lives for themselves wi" be strongly influenced by their degree of control over management. Ir a sentence—workers in a publicly owned and controlled industry can st ₁ be exploited and pushed around as " units of labour."

On the assumption that those discussing this matter will be willing to agree within the above terms of reference, this paper will make brief statements on the following topics:—

1. An appraisal of the industry.
2. Labour relations in the industry.
3. The application of Workers' Control.

The State of the Motor Industry

The industry's contribution to the economy is summarised in paragraphs 2 and 3 of the Employers' evidence to the Royal Commission:

2. " The Industry's contribution to the Gross National Product of £28,910 million in 1964 has been estimated at 3 per cent. from a labour force of approximately 485,000, or less than 2 per cent. of the working population. The Industry's exports of £942.7 million in 1964 represented 16.6 per cent. of the United Kingdom total of £4,471 million—by far the largest contribution from any identifiable

industry. We might also add that its involuntary contribution to the Exchequer in the form of motor taxation is formidable—£887 million in 1964-65, or 10.9 per cent. of the total Revenue."

3. " During the past 10 years the Industry has more than doubled its output to 2½ million vehicles in 1964 (including cars, commercial vehicles and tractors), supported by an average capital investment over the same period of £100 million per year. Of the 1,867,000 cars produced over the last year, 679,000, or 36 per cent. were exported, and in the region of 1,175,000 cars were sold on the home market. With 169,000 commercial vehicles and 157,000 tractors, the export total was over one million vehicles—nearly 60 per cent. higher than ten years earlier. The Country's vehicle exports now stand at about 22 per cent. of the total world vehicle exports. We can also expect the industry's production to continue to expand in the future, albeit at a slower pace than during the past five years. The industry itself estimated in the National Plan that home demand in 1970 will be for 1.6 million cars, based on an annual growth until then of 4.6 per cent. compared with 9.8 per cent in recent years, whilst exports may increase at the rate of 5 per cent. per year. Thus, annual car output may reach 2.3 million by 1970, with : domestic car population in that year of 12.6 million compared with 8.5 million in 1964."

Most of the figures relate to the firms submitting the evidence—B.M.C., Ford, Jaguar, Leyland, Pressed Steel, Rootes, Rover, Vauxhall—the assembly firms in fact. But it is important to realise the industry's export claim includes parts and accessories (including tyres and tubes): £226 million; agricultural tractors: £92 million in 1965, which with the other items left the export of cars and commercial vehicles at £338 million.

Components Industry

These export figures require a comment on the size and importance of the components section. On June 2nd, 1967, the " Times Business Review " quoted a spokesman for these firms, who claimed a labour force of 350,000 and a gross annual output value £800 million—and who complained bitterly of the Government's ignorance of this less easily defined area of the motor industry. An extract from the " Times 300 " for 1966 (the 300 largest firms ranked in order of capital employed) gives an indication of the relative importance of the two areas.

Rank	Comp.	£000's Cap.Emp	Net Profit before Int & Tax £000's Latest	% of Cap–Emp Latest	£000's Turnover Total	Export	Employees	£s. profit per Emp
13	Ford	211,068	10,863	5.4	383,000	152,000	61,000	178.08
36	B.M.H.	167,381	23,313	19.7	483,526	146,000	134,239	233.13
39	Leylands	138,476	20,824	21.8	215,000	71,500	68,600	367.92
52	Vauxhall	92,218	18,774	22.6	195,009	79,579	33,022	568.53
83	Rootes	71,593	Loss 413				25,000+	
	For B.M.H. and Leyland a re-classification is now necessary.							
19	Dunlop	190,599	23,623	13.2	340,000	23,750	106,100	222.65
61	Lucas	72,903	9,359	13.4	174,800		65,000	143.98
69	Rolls Royce	71,697	8,198	11.7	106,392	39,672	47,141	173.90
150	Smiths	28,732	4,395	17.7	53,300	7,460	23,800	184.66
163	Goodyear	26,126	2,772	12.8				
204	Birmid	20,552	4,857	24.7	39,319	1,400	12,000	404.75
244	Pirelli	16,614	2,373	16.1	26,516	1,800	5,430	437.02
249	W. Breedon	16,217	1,845	11.8	26,765	1,320	10,200	180.88
256	Auto Lockheed prods.	15,708	3,459	24.7	35,624			
280	Serck	13,216	1,809	18.1	15,698	2,295	5,000	361.81

The figures for the car firms are amended to include recent amalgamations, but the figures for the component firms do not indicate what proportions of capital, work force, profits, etc. are attributable solely to the manufacture of car components. And many smaller firms are excluded—e.g., Rubery Owen, Hardy Spicer and Girling.

Here, then, is a vast and complex industry. What is happening inside it? How well is it " serving the nation "?

Take-Overs—Concentration of Ownership

Ruthless international competition and the scale and cost of investment programmes are providing the motive for rapid concentration. With Fords, Vauxhall and Rootes effectively controlled by American parents, B.M.C. and Leyland have expanded through vertical and horizontal integration: B.M.C. has become B.M.H. with three separate divisions—B.M.C., Pressed Steel-Fisher and Jaguar Cars, and has sold the Pressed-Steel Linwood factory to Rootes for £14.5 million. Leyland have added the Rover-Alvis lines to their Standard Triumph car range. Recently, further talks between B.M.H. and Leyland (ostensibly about co-operative marketing moves) give weight to the belief that a merger is very possible. In the words of the " Times " correspondent Clifford Webb (June 1st, 1967) the Government, in the guise of the Industrial Reorganisation Co-operation, is " waiting eagerly in the background to step in if the going gets rough." Progress in amalgamation continues throughout the industry. G.K.N. have recently had their attempt to establish a crankshaft supply monopoly, by acquiring Birfields, referred to the Monopolies Commission. Scope for further vertical integration by the car firms is obviously considerable. Some estimate that over 60 per cent. of the finished car is " bought in " from other firms.

We can only indicate the size and nature of the structural problem. The Employers' Evidence puts it this way:—

" As far as the organisation of the Industry is concerned, the technique of mass production is widely used, designed to secure maximum benefit from the economies of large-scale manufacture. The flow line of production extends from the steel mills to the docks, with a vulnerability to disruption proportional to the delicacy of its balance. In the vehicle assembly areas particularly, the process depends on the maintenance of an adequately trained and highly interdependent labour force, serviced by a flow of parts and materials mostly by conveyor systems. Because of the manual assembly work involved, the quality of relationships engendered by the supervision is all-important. Motor manufacture also relies on very close integration with other Companies supplying components and services and the transport of finished products, so that loss of output at any stage, whether within motor manufacturing firms or supplying companies, can have very widespread repercussions. When we consider also the seasonal nature of motor car sales, the rapidity of technological change in the industry's methods and materials and the pressure of international competition, the work situation calls for the utmost co-operation on all sides. The proper observance of Procedure Agreements for resolving disputes is therefore at a high premium."

Performance: Is It Serving The Nation Well?

Output and export performance of the industry can only be gauged by comparison with the motor industries of other countries:—

Country	Date	Cars	Exp. %	Comm. Vehicles	Exp. %	Total	Exp. %
U.K.	1965	1722045	36	455216	36	2177261	36
	1960	1352728	42	457972	32	1810700	40
Canada	1965	710711	11	144765	8	855476	10
	1960	325752	5	70569	5	396321	5
France	1965	1423078	34	218218	17	1641296	32
	1960	1175301	42	193909	33	1369210	41
W. Germany	1965	2733732	52	242745	45	2976477	51
	1960	1816779	48	238370	49	2055149	48
Japan	1965	696176	14	1179438	8	1875614	10
	1960	165094	4	316457	4	481551	4
Italy	1965	1134444	27	71616	27	1206060	27
	1960	595907	33	48710	12	644617	32
Sweden	1965	181755	46	23818	58	205573	48
	1960	108302	45	20145	57	128527	47
U.S.A.	1965	9305556	1*	1751805	4*	11057366	2*
	1960	6674796	2	1194475	17	7819271	4

* Figures not comparable

These figures indicate that the industry has not expanded rapidly enough, either in terms of total output or in contribution to exports. British vehicles are losing ground in the world export markets. These facts are the more disturbing in that they apply to the key growth industry—and to an industry in which Britain has not suffered the disadvantage of an " early start "—the technological handicap arising from the burden of outdated capital equipment.

Here, then, is a key industry which is not serving the nation well. It is in danger of American domination. It needs considerable Government assistance to solve its problems. It tries to do too many things (sell too many models) and it has grave structural weakness.

Rapid Rationalisation Required

Car manufacture is oligopolistic: it is controlled by five large firms, between which collusion is a very practical possibility. Efficiency and costs would seem to dictate further concentration; presumably with the blessing of the Industrial Reorganisation Corporation. Foreign control of 50 per cent. of the industry would still be a reality, and the key significance of the industry to the national economy is not likely to diminish in the near future. All things considered, here would appear to be the top priority subject for nationalisation.

The case for public ownership is greatly enhanced by the great difficulty the private industry has had in co-ordinating the components sector with the assembly process. Vertical integration has progressed only slowly. Although there are outstanding cases in the integration of Briggs, Fisher & Ludlow, S.U. Carburettors, Pressed Steel, etc., the long and vulnerable lines of supply need to be shortened and strengthened. This appears economically viable only on a national scale.

Technological Change

Despite the claims of the employers, technological change would not seem to be a major problem for the industry. Apart from increased mechanisation in the handling of materials and the increased use of power tools, there has been little change in the methods of assembly in the last decade. Automation did revolutionise the machining of engines, and increasingly effective mechanisation has changed the nature of some types of pressing, forging and casting.

Vehicle production is still highly dependent on intensively organised groups of workers. The co-operation of these workers is therefore vital to efficient production—and the opportunity to exercise that co-operation is a basic human right. This leads directly to a consideration of industrial relations in the motor industry.

Labour Relations

Disputes in the car industry show the same trend and pattern as those exhibited by the engineering sector, and by most sectors of the economy, with the significant exception of the declining industries, e.g., coal and textiles. Vehicles appear to lead rather than follow the trend of the last decade towards more strikes, and more days lost. Lord Devlin's report on the Port Transport Industry (Cmnd. 2734) gave the following table:—

MAN-DAYS LOST IN SEVEN MAJOR INDUSTRIES

	Annual average number of Man-days lost through disputes			Average number of Man-days lost yearly in disputes per thousand insured persons		
	1930/38	1947/55	1956/64	1930/38	1947/55	1956/64
Docks	39800	344400	169100	285	3134	1091
Shipbuilding and Shiprepairing	54200	194100	514600	328	890	2349
Coalmining	1002600	616100	444000	1034	778	627
Engineering and Vehicles	88000	441700	1290300	80	162	411
Construction	71600	87900	172000	60	69	110
Textiles	1504000	21000	27100	1311	22	30
Food, Drink & Tobacco	5400	12000	22400	10	15	27

The theme is elaborated by Prof. Turner as quoted by Cliff & Barker[1]

" As one expert Professor Turner has noted:

'If one takes . . . the five year period up to 1961 one finds that the number of workers reported to have been involved in strikes is comparable with that in the five years of unrest up to and including 1926—the year of the General Strike itself; and that the number of separate strikes reported is very much higher than for any comparable period since figures first began to be systematically collected, in the 1890s.' "

And furthermore

" ' If one puts mining aside as the special case it is, the frequency of strikes for all other industries over the past few years immediately shows a very different aspect. And this is so marked that it is worth detailing. For ten years up to 1956 the reported annual number of stoppages fluctuated around 500 (which was also pretty similar to the rate for the immediate pre-war years). In 1956 itself, it was 570; but the number then rose:

In 1957 to 640, in 1958 to 670, in 1959 to 780, in 1960 to 1,180, and in 1961 to 1,220.' Continuing these figures from the point at which Turner left off we find: 1962—1,244, 1963—1,082, 1964—1,456, 1965—1,496

In other words from 1956 to 1965 the number of strikes recorded by the Ministry of Labour nearly trebled."

"Downers"

Even figures such as these fail to give the full details of what is happening. They do not take into account the hundreds of "downers" which occur in the car industry each year, but which are too short in duration to be compiled in the official statistics. They are none-the-less a very important fact of life for the car worker and the industry.

Statistics which are available do confirm the motor industry to be the most strike-prone in the manufacturing sector.

Inside the industry, no clear pattern emerges. No seasonal pattern, no geographical pattern, no group pattern. Sometimes it is the Paint Shop, sometimes the Inspectors, then it's a track group and then the delivery drivers. Stacker trucks and stores, trim and rectification, very few groups have not "had a go." Vauxhalls In Luton was for a long time the exception, and it may have been the isolation and dominance of the firm in Luton which explained the exclusion from the pattern—or it may have been the operation of the elected Management Advisory Council.

This pattern of strike activity seems peculiar to the British car industry. Some enquiry into cause is necessary. A detailed analysis of the causes in the motor industry has been made by Turner, Clack and Roberts in **Labour Relations in the Motor Industry,** pages 76 and 334. (Publisher Allen & Unwin.)

CAUSATION OF CAR FIRM DISPUTES, 1921-64	% of all strikes	of striker-days
Straight wage demands, or wage reductions	11	15
Wage Structure and workloads	44	35
Working hours and conditions	7	2
Individual dismissals	9	7
Redundancy, short time etc.	10	16
Management questions	6	6
Trade Union Relations	13	19
	100	100

LABOUR RELATIONS IN THE MOTOR INDUSTRY
Table XI/I—Car firms striker-days by cause (for the establishments involved)

000's	Inter-war (1921-39)	Post-war (1946-64)
Straight wage increase demands or reductions	100	400
Wage Structure and Workloads	150	900
Trade Union Relations, etc.		600
Redundancy, Short Time	50	600
Individual Dismissals, etc.		250
Management questions		200
Working hours and conditions		100
TOTALS	300	3000

Comparison of vehicles with other main industry groups, confirms the motor industry as being the most strike-prone, taking into account the size of the labour force. Such a comparison, detailed in Appendix XIX p. 74 of the Ministry of Labour's evidence to the Royal Commission, also indicates a somewhat higher proportion of strikes, in the motor industry, arising out of "wage disputes," "employment and discharge" and "working arrangements, rules and discipline."

Cause of Strikes

Turner, Clack and Roberts have contributed a very valuable analysis of this subject in their book "Labour Relations in the Motor Industry." In seeking any factors which might have a causal connection with the unique incidence and pattern of strikes in the British motor industry, they eliminate most of the commonly supported reasons by showing these factors to have equal bearing on other industries, and other motor industries, without producing similar results. All the theories are examined—the nature of track work, green labour, lack of Union control, complexity of payments systems, lack of devolution of managerial authority, group piece-work, high labour turnover, etc.—and found wanting in some respects. Two factors are found to stand out as being of peculiar significance in the situation: (a) The large and frequent fluctuations in levels of earnings (related to the systems of payment) and (b) the insecurity arising from (i) seasonal fluctuations in demand, and (ii) Governmental manipulation of demand. With this one real exception, by no means experienced only in the car industry, the general conclusion is there are no factors in the situation which, by themselves, determine the level of strike activity. From this the deduction is that car workers decide to strike for any one of a number of reasons which seem sufficiently urgent to warrant the stoppage.

This book is of great interest and value. It may be that too little emphasis is given to two other direct influences upon the industry's labour relations:—

1. Inefficient authoritarian management—unskilled in its ability to cope with conflict situations.
2. The maturity of the labour force in organisation and bargaining—the high built-in level of expectations and the quality of resistance to arbitrary decision-making. In itself this is a form of workers control.

Application of Workers Control

Groups throughout the industry have secured a measure of Workers' Control in their own situations. Good organisation has achieved part control in such areas as manning, track speeds, movement of labour, work loads, job evaluation, and even in the management citadel of "hiring and firing." There is no wish here to overstate the case, but in certain sections of the industry works committees and shop stewards' bodies have, through continuous bargaining, built up a deep understanding of the internal organisation of the firm, and the external problems of the industry as a whole.

At the rank and file level, the workers have through hard experience come to be familiar with the internal and external problems influencing their jobs and income. The thousands of meetings to thrash out sectional or group policies on all management attitudes—these have an educational by-product in the awareness of the complexity of organisation and the conflicting interests involved.

Given the "ripeness" of the industry and the work-force for a system of Workers' Control, what control structure would be appropriate?

With the comparatively few large units involved the system of government could be simple. The area of government would depend on the amount of the components industry brought into a publicly owned motor industry.

A National Council for the Motor Industry composed of delegates elected from National Product Councils—i.e., National Councils for Cars, 'Buses, Commercial Vehicles, Bodies, Engines, Instruments, Tyres and other product electorates. Members of these N.P.Cs. would be delegated from the Works Councils of the factories which are principally concerned with the particular product. Problems of demarcation would not be insurmountable.

Car works at least are reasonably conveniently sectionalised to form constituencies for the election of Works' Councils. Tool rooms, body shops, maintenance groups, track sections, stores, cleaners, transport groups, clerical workers, draughtsmen, etc., would all be represented through "weighted" proportional representation. Workers Councils may normally meet weekly, while the Executive Board elected from its members may need to be full-time.

Whereas a National Council would represent the whole industry in relations with the government and the rest of the economy, and have responsibility for the national investment programme, research and development, manpower and training, the export organisation, and the co-ordination of the Product Groups, the N.P.C.s would represent the difficulties, the requirements and the grievances of their members to the co-ordinating body.

Workers' Councils would retain control of the organisation of production and systems of work, systems of payment and incentives, disbursement of the works surplus, some research and training, and relations with regional planning organisations, etc.

There is no desire here to avoid the implications of public ownership without which Workers' Control is not a likely starter. Public ownership means that the state will have the authority to determine the place of the industry in the national economy, and to determine how much of its surplus the industry will retain for investment, research and as income for its workers. Workers Control on the other hand will ensure that the industry and its workers have their interests constantly promoted in the working out of national economic policy—and that the "bargaining position" is maintained and improved.

It may be that to "sell" widespread public ownership to the nation's workers, it must be nationalisation **WITH** Workers' Control. Other forms of nationalisation have not given the workers the new relationship with management, the security and the job satisfaction which we hoped would develop.

No "pie in the sky" image should come from this paper. It is just an attempt to fit the workers' control debate into the conditions prevailing in one industry and to indicate the relationship between Workers Control and the function of the trade unions. At present, the most important task is to keep alive the consciousness of the real problem of control through the organised militancy of the car workers.

With any system of control there will still be conflict between groups and the state, between groups in the economy and in the industry. There will still be alienation. There is no quick and easy path out of a jungle of attitudes which has grown in centuries of capitalist development. The path will be hacked in untidy fashion—so long as we don't go in a circle—but the prospects outside the jungle look good, and anyway, we have to keep moving or be eaten.

Incomes Policy, Legislation, and Shop Stewards. p. 81.

MOTOR CONTROL NEEDED
A paper submitted by Walter Kendall.

Just prior to the 1964 contract negotiations several large Detroit locals of the United Automobile Workers of America initiated a unique bumper sticker campaign. In all cities across the country where U.A.W. plants were located, the bumpers of auto workers' cars carried the slogan "Humanise Working Conditions." Lacking the support of official union leaders, the workers were attempting to inform the public that their chief contract objective would be to improve the conditions of factory life rather than wages. In the 1967 contract negotiations which are to begin shortly, production workers will have a similar objective in mind. The signs suggest that the 70 per cent. of locals which went out on wildcat strikes following the 1955 contract, may well be approached again in 1967.

The preoccupation with production workers' problems is a real one and is emphasised by many active militants and shop stewards here in the world motor capital of Detroit. The preoccupation is too, an international one, as is very ably documented by the recently published and most valuable British study " Labour Relations in the Motor Industry."[1]

At the end of their highly competent study of labour relations in motors the authors conclude what most of us as trade unionists know already: " We are driven to the conclusion that strikes in the motor industry have been caused mainly by the kind of pressures that strikers themselves give as reasons for striking—car firm strikes have had their roots in a pattern or complex of conscious grievances (in) which one can see that they might very well, applied to oneself, for instance, be an adequate motive for action." Such a statement from a profession hitherto noted only for its activity as ideologists for the ruling class is highly noteworthy. Its authors ought to be commended. Its text should be hung ten feet high across the plant buildings of B.M.C., Ford, Vauxhall, S.T.I., Jaguar and the other firms involved.

Strikes in British Motors have increased as follows:—

1921–1930	1931–39	1940–44	1945–49	1950–54	1955–59	1960–64
84,000 (striker days)	226,000	276,000	302,000	684,000	821,000	1,161,000*

TOTAL: 1921-1964: 3,733,000
(*Still less than 2 hours per employee per year. Capitalist press, please note)

Contrary to the still surviving adherents of Butskellism and defeatism in our movement, industrial unrest has mounted precisely as living standards have improved. Strikes are, in an era of full employment, less about simple wage issues, more about citizen rights, human dignity and decent treatment on the job. British car workers, like those in Detroit, are lining up under the slogan "Humanise Working Conditions." The following table of strike causes illustrates the point:—

Car Firm Striker Days	1921–39	1946–64
Wage Increase or Decrease ...	100	400
Wage Structure, Work Loads	150	900
T.U. Relations, etc.		600
Redundancy, Short time, etc.		600
Individual Dismissals	50	250
Management Questions		200
Working Hours & Conditions		100
	300	3000

The major portion of motor industry disputes, as this table indicates, are caused by shop floor initiatives seeking encroachment on managerial prerogative. What these figures express is a spontaneous determination to transfer an important range of decisions out of the dictatorial hands of arbitrary management into the firm grip of the organised working class.

Motor industry stewards and militants have embarked on the road towards industrial democracy without yet fully realising the fact.

To quote our "neutral" academics, "In the interwar period . . . work place organisations were mainly preoccupied with the struggle to maintain wages—and labour standards—in the face of persistent mass unemployment. With memories of the interwar period diminished . . . the horizon of labour expectations lifted." "This change in expectations seems best expressed in two ideas or beliefs, the idea that wages should be "fair" in competitive terms; and the idea that performance of a job establishes property rights in it."

Translated out of the jargon, what does this mean? Firstly it is a statement that about wages the shop stewards have been more often right than the bosses. Management as a whole have no clear conception of why they are paying, what they are paying for, and what they get. As a result massive irrationalities and inequalities in wage structure exist both within individual firms, especially B.M.C., and between company units in the whole. Shop steward wages demands, in short, have been directed to teaching incompetent labour management its own job. Secondly, to the extent that shop stewards and workers insist on "fair wages" where time work is involved, particularly "on the line," they are directly challenging management-claimed prerogative to allocate work loads dictatorially and as it pleases. In one field therefore shop stewards pressure is designed to introduce equity and rationality into an irrational and inequitable wages structure, thus disputing management competence and prerogative indirectly, whilst in the other it does so head on.

As to "job rights," let the university gentlemen explain for themselves, which they do very well. "The concept of 'job property rights' has far reaching implications—it extends not merely to the sense that operatives should not be turned off en masse ('lay-offs' to you, K.) when it is no longer profitable to employ them, or that the individual worker should not be deprived of his property rights established by service without appeal—it also includes the idea of rights to a particular job at a particular place, and may extend to the right to consultation in anything which may affect the future value of his 'property' . . . In effect, the pursuit of 'fair wages' in detail and the protection and elaboration of 'job property rights' have become, even though these principles are rarely consciously expressed as principles of its operation, the central business of union work shop negotiations and the emotional basis of its strength."

The significance of all this to those of us, workers and intellectuals, attending this workers' control conference ought to be self evident. Down there below, in those irredeemable depths of ignorance, and spontaneity, regularly condemned by both "revolutionary" sectarians and petty bourgeois socialists, the workers already have the idea and are putting it into practice although not yet at a theoretically clarified level. At the present time the real bargaining table is that at which sit the shop stewards in the factory not that at which sit union and employers' leaders at York. That being so, it should be one of the foremost aims of our conference to examine ways and means of bringing a higher rationality into the existing spontaneous motor workers' demands for encroaching control. Motor workers represented at Coventry should most seriously consider producing a leaflet or pamphlet which can be circulated in thousands inside the plants, developing, amplifying and illustrating the points made herein. Such a pamphlet would find as ready a market in Detroit as in Cowley and Birmingham. A shop stewards' movement for industrial democracy in motors can, and should be, put on foot.

All the evidence suggests that the time is ripe for action on both tactical and strategical scales. Tactical, by formulating explicit worked-out demands which can be incorporated in day-to-day industrial bargaining. Strategically, by motor workers themselves formulating specific proposals for industrial democracy, workers self-management of **the plants and of the industry as a whole.** Motor workers are at present working for, organising for, striking for an extension of industrial democracy into the work place without realising fully what it is. Is it too much to expect that our conference will take practical and positive steps to make this implicit demand explicit, to transfer it from the realm of a half understood longing to a fully worked out, rational, negotiable and achievable, **political** demand?

[1] **Labour Relations in the Motor Industry.** Turner, Clack and Roberts. Allen & Unwin 55/-.

REPORT ON MOTOR INDUSTRY SEMINAR

By Tony Topham.

The seminar consisted of over twenty workers from the car industry, mostly A.E.U. members, who represented a very wide cross-section of different firms in both the assembly and components sections.

Two papers were discussed—one from Bob Harrison, who spent three years in the industry as a shop steward, and the other from Walter Kendall of " **Union Voice** " who is at present in the American car centre of Detroit.

Both papers stressed the need to develop a workers' control movement in the industry which was based on the actual problems facing car workers— the threats to security and wages posed by rationalisation, takeovers and the declining position of the British industry in a competitive international market.

The potential for a workers' control movement is clearly revealed in the statistics of strikes, which show a rising proportion to be about matters of managerial action. The findings of academic experts have recently confirmed that car workers strike about **real** issues, about their objections to managerial authority, and about their need to control the job situation more effectively. The drives towards new methods of wage payment, such as " measured day work " were now threatening the controls which had been established by the shop-stewards in recent years.

They now faced a situation similar to that of 1956 when the struggle against redundancies had presented an opportunity (which had been missed then) to establish the demand for workers' control. However, it was generally agreed that the much more political nature of the struggle in **1967,** with the workers' control demand springing up in many industries and the labour movement itself, provided much more fruitful ground.

The principal obstacle to be overcome was the fragmented character of the car workers' militancy, but it was felt that the very nature of the workers' control demand promoted unity, since it raised a demand which was not confined to a particular factory or section. In this way the dominant sectionalism of the industry's workers could be overcome. In its turn, such a unity would link up with the struggles now impending in the docks, steel, transport and aircraft industries.

The ripeness of the industry, and of the work-force, for a system of workers' control, was therefore fully accepted by the seminar. The question therefore arose as to how this was to be expressed. It was agreed that, as Walter Kendall had written: " the workers already have the idea and are putting it into practice although not yet at a theoretically clarified level . . . that being so it should be one of the foremost aims of the conference to examine ways and means of bringing a high rationality into the existing spontaneous motor workers' demands for encroaching control." Or, as Bob Harrison says: "Groups throughout the industry have secured a measure of workers' control in their own situations. Good organisation has achieved part-control in such areas as manning, track speeds, movement of labour, work loads, job evaluation, and even in the management citadel of 'hiring and firing.'"

The next task was to make these controls firm: to insist on them as a political right, and to grow from this towards a plan for full workers' control, which would naturally raise the question of public ownership. The latter would then have to ' ε based on a democratic system of workers' councils

To this end, it was agreed that a pamphlet on workers' control in the industry should be produced, and to ask the C.S.E. to assist in its publication.

In plenary discussion later, the question of a car workers' conference was also raised. The movement has made firm beginnings at Coventry. As Bob Harrison concluded his paper:

" There is no quick and easy path out of a jungle of attitudes which has grown in centuries of capitalist development. The path will be hacked in untidy fashion—so long as we don't go in a circle—but the prospects outside the jungle look good, and anyway, we have to keep moving or be eaten."

The Bulletin of the Institute for Workers' Control
contributors include Michael Barratt-Brown, Stephen Bodington, Ken Coates, Royden Harrison, John Hughes, Bill Jones, Walter Kendall, Ian Mikardo, M.P., Ernie Roberts, Alan Rooney, Hugh Scanlon, Tony Topham and many others.

Quarterly, 96 pp.   Single issues 8/-, Annual Subscription 30/- from 91 Goldsmith Street, Nottingham.

PUBLICATIONS OF THE

INSTITUTE FOR WORKERS' CONTROL
from 91 Goldsmith Street, Nottingham.

The Way Forward for Workers' Control	Hugh Scanlon	1/6
Productivity Bargaining	Tony Topham	1/6
Labour and Sterling	M. Barratt-Brown	1/6
Opening the Books	M. Barratt-Brown	1/6
The Labour Party's Plan for Industrial Democracy	Ken Coates & Tony Topham	1/6

ARCHIVE SERIES

Student Power	Bertrand Russell	6d.
Workers' Control & Revolution	Antonio Gramsci	1/-

A Group of Sheffield Steel Workers

Steel Workers Next Step

Pamphlet series no. 7   1-6d

The Steel Industry in 1968 — A Paper from the Sheffield Steel Workers' Group

1. The Demand for Employment in Steel 1967-68

1967 was a bad year for the steel industry. Output was for the second year running more than 10% below the 1964-65 peak. Yet imports were coming in at twice the level of 1965 or 1966. Numbers employed were only slightly down on 1966 but 1966 had recorded a drop of nearly 2,000 over 1965. Within the totals employed big changes took place in 1967. Male production operatives dropped by 10,000 or by about 7%, (BISAKTA's membership fell by about 7,000); while staff and females increased by 10.000. Weekly earnings were on average £1 up on 1966, that is an increase of about 7%; but this was the result of increases for maintenance and other service workers and labourers and decreases for some process workers.

1968 has begun with redundancies being announced in Scotland, Wales and Sheffield. It seems almost certain that they must be followed by more. If the rate of growth of the economy is to be held back to 3% a year, demand for steel is unlikely to grow by much more than 5%. This increase can probably be produced with a smaller labour force, since there has been much short time working (average hours worked by process workers were still three hours a week less in 1967 than in 1964) and since productivity (output per man hour) has been rising on average by about 3% per year and can be expected to continue doing so. The major rationalisation measures being planned by the Corporation are scheduled for 1969-70, but a slower growth in the economy than expected could easily advance the threatened redundancies.

2. The Policies of the Unions

There is no doubt that the emphasis placed by the Government on increased productivity for justifying claims for higher wages will lead to Union pressure for productivity bargains on behalf of some workers even if this is at the expense of redundancies.

Already BISAKTA members are negotiating new productivity bargains in many plants. The claim of the A.E.F. for a substantial wage rise and shorter hours etc., has been largely rejected by the employers following the comments of the Prices and Incomes Board. While maintenance workers in steel now receive slightly above the national average for all engineering workers, their earnings fall much below those available in the motor car and aircraft industries. The growth of productivity bargaining at both national and plant level and the undermining of traditional piece-work bargains continue to produce a new position in wage determination in the steel industry as in engineering. As Hugh Scanlon has emphasised, no engineering worker would lament the passing of piece-work payment, so long as the principle of 'mutuality', i.e. of a bargain entered into between worker and employers is maintained; and with it the freedom of the worker to work at his own rhythm and not one set for him by measured day-work and similar schemes.

These changes in bargaining procedures require above all unity among the different unions in steel and machinery for concerting demands. Yet not only are the process men divided between BISAKTA, NUB, GMW and T&GWU, there is still no agreement on white collar representation which is being fought for by the GMW, BISAKTA and ASSET.

3. The Steel Towns in the 1970's.

The divisions amongst the Unions in steel are resulting in something else as serious as the completly unco-ordinated, and even competitive, presentation of wage demands. It is the lack of any unified policy that has created a position where redundancies are already being announced before a comprehensive procedure for plant closures and redundancies has been negotiated. These redundancies have moreover been real; jobs were not always available in other plants to replace jobs in plants closed down; and where they were it was sometimes only as a result of offering redundancy to older men in the continuing plants to make room for younger workers. So far the closures have been of single plants within a combine, as at Park Gate. The closure of whole combines, which is bound to come as rationalisation proceeds, will involve much more serious problems. The Unions must have ready a common strategy to meet this situation or they will be overwhelmed by events.

The Benson Report, produced by the BISF on the eve of steel nationalisation, suggested the following pattern of plants surviving after rationalisation, i.e. to meet demand for 32m. tons bulk steel in 1975 (i.e. excluding special steel demand for 3.3 m. tons)

A. *Integrated Works*	*Number of Works*	*Tonnage Capacity*
North Lincs.	One works	5m. tons plus
Teeside	One or two works	6m. tons plus
South Wales	Two works	8m. tons
Deeside	One works	2m. tons plus
Scotland	One works	3.3m. tons
TOTAL	6 or 7 works	24.3m. tons
B. *Scrap Using Works*		
Sheffield	One works	1—1½m. tons
S. Lancs. and Midlands	One or two works	2—3m. tons
TOTAL		4½m. tons
C. *Engineering and Tubemaking Works*		
Scattered	Four or five plants	3—2m. tons

The Benson Report emphasised that this last figure involved the elimination of some 9m. tons of capacity at 14 works belonging to the engineering and tubemaking firms.

The effect of the nationalisation of bulk steel making is to transfer to the Steel Corporation this awkward task of eliminating 14 plants from the engineering and tubemaking firms. These firms have received compensation for the plants that will be closed and can use this for their own developments wherever they wish. But the separation of bulk steel making and engineering in the process of nationalisation leaves to the Corporation a very small base for diversifying into any other activities in those areas where steel making plants are totally closed down. The prospect for many steel-making towns, where closure is indicated and there is little alternative industry, is bleak indeed. It will not be enough for the steel unions to ensure that their members are offered redundancy pay or transfer to other areas where places are made for them by early retirements, even if this were itself a real solution for the human problems involved.

If the Unions are to ensure not only employment for their older members and for those who cannot or do not wish to move house, but also employment for their children and some defence against an excess supply of steel workers in relation to demand, then they will have to ensure that new industries are developed in the areas where steel-making is to be phased out. If they leave this to foot-loose private enterprise they are doomed to disappointment. Their best hope is to press upon the Corporation the necessity for diversifying into engineering and chemicals production in these areas. The T.U.C. has already proposed that the Coal Board and the Steel Corporation should establish jointly a public agency for this purpose in those areas where both coal and steel are being run down. This will not happen unless the Steel Union and the N.U.M. make common cause to demand action along these lines. In terms of the economies of scale and of the external economies of integrated complexes of production, the fuel and power and steel industries provide the base for a number of major developments of modern industry. Nothing less than united Trade Union pressure upon the Government and upon the public corporations will achieve this result.

4. The Worker Involvement Scheme

It was announced on 28th March that the BSC had finally chosen their "worker directors". It has taken the corporation since 26th January, 1967 to draw up and announce their proposals for 'worker participation in management'. So one year and two months later we learn that 12 'employee directors' will join 10 other part-time directors on the four Group boards in order to "participate with top management in shaping the industry's policies" and "share responsibility for board decisions".

Three 'employee directors' will sit on each of the four Group boards for three years beginning 1st May. Before then they will be preparing for their new duties by attending a five-week introductory course on "top management" designed and run jointly by the BSC and the TUC. Although Lord Melchett personally chose the 12 'employee directors', he did so from a short list drawn up by the TUC from the large numbers who were nominated by their union. In most cases, these nominations were from the executives rather than from the local branch or shop floor.

The 12 'employee directors' will continue to work on the shop floor between boardroom duties and will receive £1,000 a year on top of their normal pay which averages about £1,000. In addition, they will be paid expenses and compensation for loss of earnings. These directors must serve their boards in a personal capacity and relinquish all union offices during their term as a director. Although the BSC underlines the point that directors have not been appointed as representatives of their trades or trade union, it is not clear as to whether a director, if he so wished, could continue to attend his local branch and report on his activities. If an 'employee director' were to do so, then it is more than likely that the BSC would demand adherance to the principles of 'board secrecy' and 'corporate responsibility'.

Part-time Members of the Group Boards

Midland Group

A. R. Hay — Chairman and Managing Director of Naylor, Benzon & Co., London (ore merchants); ex-United Steel director.

H. Smith — Chairman and Managing Director of British Ropes, Doncaster; ex-United Steel director.

Sir Roger Stevens — Vice-Chancellor of Leeds University; chairman of Yorkshire and Humberside Economic Planning Council; ex-Ambassador to Sweden and Persia.

Jack Surman (44) — Second vessel man, LD/AC steel making plant, Normanby Park steelworks, Scunthorpe; local councillor since 1952 and Mayor of Scunthorpe in 1966. Member of Lysaght's Joint Works Committee for many years and chairman for 1967.

John Walton (40) — Shunter, Appleby-Frodingham, Scunthorpe. Union delegate for the Traffic Department Lodge of the NUB, of which, for the last four years he has been chairman of the North Midlands district delegate board and national executive member. Scunthorpe councillor. Ex-Sheffield University day-release student.

Stanley Waring (55) — Stockyard foreman, Steel, Peech & Tozer, Rotherham. Secretary of a foreman and supervisors branch of BISAKTA.

Northern and Tubes

C. R. Chetwynd (51) — Deputy Chairman, Land Commission; former director of the North East Development Council.

J. Slater (57) — Assistant manager of a finishing mill, Dorman Long's Lackenby Works, Middlesbrough.

L. Eaton (47) — Chief clerk, Stanton & Staveley Works, nr. Nottingham.

Joe O'Hagan (66) — Ex-NUB general secretary; TUC General Council and chairman 1966.

Jock Kane (42) — Chargehand blast furnaceman, Corby Works, Steward & Lloyds, Corby.

Scottish and North West Group

W. L. Mather — Chairman, Mather & Platt, Manchester

Rt. Hon Viscount Muirshiel of Milmacolm, formerly John Maclay, Conservative Secretary of State, Scotland). Director of P & O.

Edward Griffiths (39) — Industrial chemist, Shotton Works, Deeside.

James Morrison (47) — Bricklayer, Lanarkshire Steelworks, Colvilles, Motherwell.

Cyril Whur (52) — Roughing rollerman, Lancashire Steelworks, Irlam. Branch secretary and national executive member of BISAKTA.

South Wales Group

Sir Hugh Weeks Director, Industrial & Commercial Finance Corporation.
Professor F. Llewellyn-Jones Principal, University College of Swansea.
James E. McComb General manager, Cwmbran Development Corporation.
W. G. Williams Shift foreman, Trostre Works.
J. F. Wiley Fitter, East Morr Works, Cardiff.
W. D. Griffiths Cold mill feeder, Ebbw Vale Steelworks.

The proposals for worker directors on each of the four Steel Group boards provides the danger of workers representation being saddled with great responsibility and little or no power. In fact, Richard Marsh sees the sharing of responsibility and the involvement of the workers, through these 'employee directors', "in the decisions which have to be made — and some of the decisions will be uncomfortable decisions" as one of the central purposes of the scheme. The more they are separated from their base in their unions and in their own works the more powerless these directors will be. Every attempt will be made to isolate them from rank and file pressures by enforced secrecy concerning board discussions and decisions, by the prerequistes of their new offices and by their removal from all union positions. To offset this, the worker directors will have to insist on sharing as much as possible of the information they acquire and on finding regular and frequent means of discussion with rank and file members and with Union committees at plant level.

5. Consultative Advisory Committees

The most important development for the future of worker control in the steel industry will be the establishment of the new system of representatives of consultative committees at different and corporation level. For these committees to develop in the direction of workers' control two principles must be established:
    a. the Committee must be elected from Trade Union nominations at each level;
    b. the Committees at each level must have representatives on them from the lower levels.

If national and group consultative advisory committees consist only of full-time union officers the possibility will be lost of bringing rank and file pressure to bear up the whole ladder of consultation and of carrying back into the lower level committees a real, appreciation of the overall policies within which plant and departmental decisions are being operated. Moreover, it is only with a system of representatives of consultative committees at different levels that the worker directors would be able to establish some real power to influence decisions at the Group Boards.

What is needed now is to create a climate of opinion which will make it possible to bring the worker directors and the whole consultative machinery in the steel industry under effective democratic control. This climate can only be created by establishing workers control groups drawn up from as many unions as possible in each of the steel plants. These groups should begin to inform themselves about the product, the management and the finance of their works and about the operations of the Corporation and its Group board. They will need to ask for opening of the Company and Corporation books, not only to protect the immediate interests of the workers and to defend them against unplanned redundancy, but in order to be able to make the necessary social demands for the best continuing contribution of the works manpower, equipment and funds to society as a whole. For all these purposes they will need to make contact with similar groups in other steel works and with workers' control groups in other industries. Out of such contacts will grow the demand for increasing social control over the economy which alone can make workers' control at the plant level effective.

29th March, 1968

Industrial Democracy

and

National Fuel Policy

Institute for Workers' Control

Pamphlet Series No. 8　　　1/6d

A MINERS' PROGRAMME
A Social Audit of the Coal Industry

NOTE: This programme is only concerned with the relations of the coal industry to the economy as a whole. It would have to be complemented by a second equally important programme of demands concerning the conditions of work in the industry. Only thus could a viable coal industry be established.

1. **The Need for Unity**

No programme of demands from the N.U.M. can have any hope of success unless it is designed to win allies for the miner's cause among other Unions and indeed througout the whole Labour Movement. Appeals to past history and sentiment are not enough. The N.U.M. could only too easily become isolated and picked off as one by one the seamen, dockers, railway men and bus men have been. The inevitable clash that can be expected between the Minister of Labour and the unions which are currently demanding wage increases, creates both the opportunity and the need for inter-union collaboration.

2. **The Tonnage Figures**

The Government November 1967 Fuel Policy White Paper states (p.66) that "The decision was taken to try to hold the demand for coal by 1970 at around 155 million tons if this was practicable and necessary". Although the Paper was withdrawn three days after issue on account of devaluation of the £, Mr. Marsh has said that "no wholesale revision of the White Paper is envisaged." For various reasons listed below it seems to be necessary to accept this figure of 155m. tons for 1970. But the cut to 120m. tons by 1975 cannot be accepted, let alone the cut to 80m. tons by 1980. The reasons for accepting the figure of 155m. tons as realistic are as follows:—

(1) Output for the year 1967-8 is likely to be around 165m. tons but stocks rose in 1967 by nearly ten million tons.

(2) Growth of the economy up to 1970 is likely to be well below the 1965 Plan target and even below the 3% p.a. predicted in the 1967 Fuel Policy.

(3) The Oil Company Refineries, the Nuclear Power Stations and the Natural Gas installations are already too far advanced, on

the basis of their expected shares of the market, to be checked now.

(4) The 155m. ton estimate is based on considerably more protection for coal in power stations than is currently being provided.

(5) The 155m. ton figure includes 24m. tons of coke ovens in 1970 that is most unlikely to be required.

The reasons for rejecting the 1975 figure include the enormous addition to the balance of payments burden of oil imports (36m. tons more than today or nearly £200 million at post-devaluation prices) and the uncertainty as to whether natural gas can be absorbed at such a fast rate as is implied by estimated sales of 49m. tons c.e. in 1975. (Only 14m. tons c.e. of gas are planned to go to power stations by 1975 and present uses of gas require only 25m. tons of coal equivalent fuel).

3. **The Nature of the Tonnage Guarantee**

Although the tonnage figure may be accepted, the nature of the guarantee "if practicable and desirable" is totally unacceptable and must be changed to a hard and fast guarantee underwritten by the Government. Nothing less can be accepted if the confidence of the men is to be regained, the rising costs of imported fuels are to be held back and the programmed development of natural gas is to be realistic. The major problem for the industry has been the succession of ever declining targets for 1970 —240—200—180—155. What matters is to get a guaranteed figure that the Government can be held to.

The Government has agreed in principle not only to maintain the 2d tax on fuel oil but to require the Electricity Generating Board and the Gas Council to use more coal than they would otherwise have done. To these measures should be added the following:—

(a) Provision of a free coal or smokeless fuel allowance to all persons over 65, to be supplied directly by the Board as with the miners' concessionary coal.

(b) Requirement of all public bodies that they use solid fuel unless a special case, including a case based on wide price differences, can be made for exemption.

(c) Development of solid fuel based district heating schemes.

(d) Rapid expansion of research into the use of coal for oil and chemicals and as the base for synthetic materials.

4. **Pricing Policy and Costs**

The costing assumptions of the statistical analysis on which the Fuel Policy White Paper was based need to be examined very closely. (The quotations are from Appendix I of the White Paper, pp. 56—64).

(a) "The quantity of Natural Gas available from the North Sea, the most economic method of absorption and its price to the gas industry". The quantity of natural gas likely to be available by 1970 was revised between January and April 1967 to twice the earlier estimate (p. 63). The price is still not determined except for one company's supplies and this was not determined when the Paper was issued. Moreover the price to the consumer depends on the load factor in the pipes and this in turn on the ability of industry and private users to absorb extra gas, taking into account the additional appliances or conversion of appliances required. On this the Paper is quite clear (Appendix II) that it is the town gas market that would give most savings but it is here that the cost of adapting appliances is greatest. Hence the need to push natural gas into power stations in order to build up an economic load for the pipes as soon as possible. Under the revised proposals that followed the Surrey Conference in May 1967 it was decided, however, to hold back the growth of gas sales to power stations. If the argument about premium sales means anything this should mean increased demand for coal not only in the power stations but as a result of relatively higher gas costs in other markets also. It is not clear, moreover, whether the estimates of coal demand for power stations include the possibility of a combination in some stations of coal and natural gas, coal being supplied in the winter months, gas in the summer.

(b) "Relative selling prices (including transport and other charges when appropriate) of the various fuels" — particularly between coal and oil. Apart from the oil tax, for which different assumptions were specifically indicated, the Paper states that "the work undertaken . . . led to the conclusion that the pattern of demand would not be greatly affected by any likely variation in these price relativities" (p: 61). But it was assumed that "oil's already appreciable advantage over coal for most uses would increase slightly" (p: 60). Such an assumption excludes the possibility of rationalising coal distribution costs or obtaining additional coal from certain pits at less than average cost.

It has become evident from the discussion of the claims of rival fuels to supply aluminium smelters in Scotland or North Wales that the Coal Board is seriously limited in its ability to charge *additional* users a price based on lowest marginal cost instead of something near average cost. The limitation arises from the rule imposed upon the Board of non-discrimination in the pricing of supplies to different coal users. The Electricity Generating Board has complained that it has been regarded as a captive market and has failed to get the benefit of lowest cost supplies available near to its power stations. There is an argument here for special prices for large users like Electricity and steel; but there is an even greater argument for special prices to *additional* users who would take output from pits which could supply large quantities at lowest cost.

(c) "The Economic rate of development of nuclear power". The Paper states (p. 61) that "Separate work on nuclear power costs made it possible to dispense with alternative assumptions as to how much nuclear power there would be by 1975 and to work on the basis that the existing programme would be fulfilled". But the Table of Generating Costs shown in Appendix III (p: 78) of the Paper purports to give figures for different fuels in the year 1967. These were all estimates since none of the stations were built then.

	1967 Estimates of Generating Costs (pence per KWh)
Nuclear	
Dungeness 'B'	0·52
Hinkley Point 'B'	0·48
Coal	
Cottam	0·53
Drax	0·56
Oil	
Pembroke with tax	0·53
without tax	0·42

The argument of the Appendix is that the costs of the next Nuclear Power Station after Hinkley will be down to the figure of stations using untaxed oil and that in any case the construction costs of conventional coal using stations will be higher in future than the figures shown here since they were based on 1964 building costs. But the crucial assumption is that coal will not be mined for power stations at an average of less than $2\frac{1}{2}$d. per therm at pit head (3d. per therm delivered). That is equivalent to about 75s. per ton delivered. In fact, it is argued that this would have to be the cost of the highest cost fuel delivered to power stations since these are the stations whose output the nuclear station would replace. It is true that coal prices for power stations ranged in 1967 between

3d. and 6d. at pit head (3½d.-6½d. delivered) with an average of 5d., but something like 25 million tons must have been already available at under 3d.; it does not seem impossible that three times that amount might be available at that price by 1975 (discounting general price increases which will hit all fuels). The White Paper assumes that only 65 million tons of coal will be provided to power stations in 1975 although added protection might allow of 72 million tons being used in 1970.

(d) "Rate of interest on new investment". On this the Paper states that "Scrutiny indicates that . . . within accepted limits (this) was unlikely to have any significant effect on the demand forecasts". Reworking of the relative costs of nuclear and coal fired power stations on an 8% D.C.F. basis would probably be much more favourable to coal. The following calculations are taken from R. W. Bates and M. G. Webb "Government Control over Investment Planning in Nationalised Electricity Supply Industry" *Bulletin* of the Oxford University Institute of Economics and Statistics, February 1968.

Type of Station	Generating Costs	
	Based upon 6% discount rate per KWh.	Based upon 8% discount rate per KWh.
Nuclear	0·6d.	0·9d.
Coalfired	0·7d.	0·8d.

(e) "Certain additional factors were considered and particularly the possibility that money costs may not be an accurate measure of cost to the nation." This refers to the social costs of unemployment and unused resources in mining areas where pits are closed. Although the White Paper says that this concept of social costs has been "an important aid in reaching decisions" (p. 62), it is not clear what weight, if any, was put on this factor. The main argument, as has been shown, was in terms of money costs. What is more there is little or no indication that thought has been given to the possibility of developing a truly integrated fuel policy which made use of new technical possibilities, such as the use of the heat generation in nuclear power stations for carbon distillation.

The conclusion of this section must be that the N.U.M. should demand:

(a) Independent review of the Fuel Policy asumptions and estimates by a special unit consisting of economists, engineers and accountants, set up under the auspices of the Select Committee on Nationalised Industries.

(b) The nationalisation of natural gas and oil exploration and production in the British Isles and territorial waters.
(c) An Energy Authority to work out an integrated plan for all fuel and power sources and to administer such a plan subject to review by the unions involved in the fuel and power industries.

5. Manpower Rundown

If we accept Lord Roben's figures, the manpower cuts involved from 1967 to 1971 by Area will be as follows:

	1967	1971	% Cut 1967-71	Compare % Cut 1963-7
Great Britain	391,000	282,000	28	23
Yorkshire	93,000	78,000	17	16
Northern	75,000	48,000	36	30
East Midlands	72,500	59,000	19	16
Wales	57,400	39,000	32	29
Scotland	39,700	25,000	37	27
West Midlands	28,000	21,000	24	23
North West	20,900	7.000	67	25
South East	4,000	4,000	0	12

In all cases the *rate* of decline between 1967 and 1971 will be greater than in the last four years and that was considerably greater than in the previous four years.

The manpower figure predicted for 1975 on the assumption of a fall in output to 120 million tons would increase the rate of decline for 1971-75 to quite unmanageable proportions (40% nationally and higher figures still in Yorkshire and the East Midlands). What is involved is a cut of over 100,000 men in each of the two four year periods. It is true that 90,000 were cut in the four years 1963-7 but only at the expense of grave collapse of confidence and sharp falls in productivity in 1965 when boom employment conditions outside the industry attracted men away from the most productive pits. The same situation could recur; but immediately the seriousness of the cuts is due to the high levels of unemployment in the very areas where pits are to be closed. This is now true not only in South Wales (unemployed in Rhondda is 8%, in Bishop Auckland 7% and in Irvine 6%) but in South Yorkshire (unemployment in Thorne is 9% and in Mexborough 4·5 %) and in the Midlands (Nuneaton 4·3%).

It is necessary to insist on the principle that pits should not be closed without provision of suitable alternative employment. This demand needs to be spelled out in a quite specific way, so that it becomes a matter for agreement between the N.C.B. and the N.U.M. whether suitable employment does or does not exist.

6. The Demand for Information

It has been an ironical experience of joint consultation in the coal industry that detailed accounts for colliery and area operations have only been forthcoming from the Coal Board when they were required to justify a pit closure. Nevertheless in certain areas — North Derbyshire is an example — the provision of such information in the event of closures has been extended to a much more regular and fuller statement of the financial position to both pit and area consultatives prior to final decisions being made. Detailed costings are not easy to master and are still more difficult to relate to wider considerations of sales policy, investment criteria etc. The demand must be pressed forward for more effective communication between national, area and pit levels of consultations and for wider circulation of documents. The establishment of the audit unit proposed some years ago should be put forward again — to operate under the Select Committee on Nationalised Industries as a body to which appeal could be made against Board decisions with which the Union could not agree.

7. **The Right to Work**

The traditional claim of the N.U.M. and of other Unions which sent representatives to Parliament to make good their claim was to the elementary right to work. There are not only 300,000 more unemployed today than in July 1966, there are altogether 750,000 less at work than in that month, because another 450,000 women and older men have not registered for jobs. To offer men at 55 three years pay and the hand-shake is to create demoralisation and despair and to lose to society the services of many who are willing and desirous to continue working and earning a decent wage.

There are five alternatives that could be offered to men as "suitable" employment.

(a) Work at the same rate at another pit not more than 20 miles away and with transport provided and a five year guarantee of employment.

(b) Work at the same rate in another pit more than 20 miles way with a house and removal expenses provided and a ten year guarantee of employment.

(c) Retraining and something near full pay at a local retraining centre for a new trade in which there are likely to be available jobs.

(d) Work within a 20 mile radius in a different industry at comparable rates of pay.

(e) Temporary work for the local authority subsidised by government on schemes of building and renewal at the local rate for the job and on the assumption that this was preparatory to wider job opportunities that were being created.

8. New Developments in the Public Sector

Employment for men in coal, on the railways, in gas, water and electricity undertakings and in the steel industry amounted in 1960 to 11½% of all male employment. By 1971 this may be expected to have fallen to 7½% given the present proposals for reducing the mining industry and rationalising steel. This reduction of public sector employment may be resisted but new employment will have to be in much less labour intensive industries than coal and the railways have been. Very large quantities of capital will therefore be required for producing employment for something like two-thirds of a million men. But it is precisely a highly capitalised public sector of science-based industries that the government needs in order to strengthen its control over the economy and that Mr. Wilson promised in his Election Speeches that Labour would establish.

The nationalised industries of coal and steel and electricity and gas (to which oil should be added) also provide the basis for a public super-holding company that would not only integrate the plans of the whole steel, fuel and power sector but would be able to diversify into a wide range of secondary industries. Such a proposal has already been accepted in principle by the T.U.C. General Council in its recent Economic Report. What is now needed is a powerful demand from the N.U.M. in association with the Transport and General and the A.E.U. for its detailed implementation.

There is no hope that the problem of re-employing redundant miners can be solved by attracting small footloose firms into mining areas, nor even by extending schemes of local building and renewal. These must be associated with major developments of the public sector in each of the old mining areas around the growing points of steel and coal and chemicals and in relation to road and rail transport and the deep water ports.

9. A New Economic Plan

Neither a guaranteed fuel policy nor the development of public sector employment can be effective except as part of a new economic plan involving the complete reversal of the disastrous Tory policies of the last three years. What is required is a plan that "discriminates ruthlessly in the interests of Labour's priorities," as Mr. Wilson promised in the Spring of 1964. Only by the government using discriminatory control over investment and foreign trade can full employment and rising living standards for workers be combined with a balance of foreign payments. The miners have the greatest interest in both full employment and a discriminatory fuel policy but the rest of the Labour Movement has an almost equal interest in such policies. The N.U.M. still has both the political strength in Parliament and the economic strength in the T.U.C. — not to act alone to defend its members — but to lead both the political and economic wings of the Labour Movement in demanding a total change of Government policy back to the principles on which it was elected and forward to Socialism.

10. A Special Session of the Labour Party Conference

The resolution passed in December by the Yorkshire Area Council of the N.U.M. may be taken as expressing the final demand of the miners that making the necessary changes in the Government's economic policy be regarded as a matter of the greatest urgency, calling for an emergency session of the Labour Party Conference.

FUEL POLICY
Resolution from Bullcroft Branch

This Council meeting of the N.U.M. Yorkshire Area instructs the National Executive Committee of the N.U.M. to call upon the National Executive Committee of the Labour Party; in conformity with Clause VI paragraph 1 of the Party Constitution to convene a special session of the Party Conference.

It insists that the White Paper on Fuel Policy has created an emergency: an unprecedented crisis of confidence has arisen between the miners, the working class, the Party and the electorate on the one hand, and the Government on the other. The White Paper is not a special, parochial concern for the miners alone: with large pools of unemployment throughout our country and the broken promises of the Government of the day, makes it the concern of the whole Labour Movement.

It recognises that it would not be a national emergency to have a planned run-down of mining manpower within the context of the promised end of "Stop Go" and the expansion of the economy on the basis of a 4% growth rate. It declares that it is a national emergency when mining manpower is to be run down at the rate of 35,000 jobs a year in the context of the abandonment of the National Plan: falling investment and manufacturing out-put: rising unemployment: and wages under severe restraint.

It reminds the National Executive Committee of the Labour Party that it was the miners who put this Party on the map and gave it some of its greatest leaders, from Keir Hardie to Nye Bevan. We have a special claim upon the loyalty of all organisations affiliated to the Party, but we ask for nothing for ourselves only that the pledges made by the Government be honoured: full employment: Planned Growth of the Economy including a dynamic and fully costed fuel plan.

The National Executive Committee of the Labour Party must convene a special session of the Party Conference so that the Government is blown back on to course and the will of the Party and the Electorate fairly and freely asserted.

The Miners' Demands and Union Strategy by Lawrence Daly

What should the miners do in face of the Coal Board's argument?

It is not a new one. Indeed it was used by the private coalowners throughout the entire period of their ownership. Improved wages and conditions could not be afforded. Reforms were ruinous. Our competitors would steal our markets! The whip of unemployment reinforced the "logic". If our forefathers had accepted these contentions no improvements would ever have been made.

When moderation in policy and strategy is advocated within our own ranks this also is nothing new. It had its advocates before nationalisation and also when the Tories were in Power between 1951 and 1964. It is not advocated only when a Labour Government is in power. But the election of a Labour Government gives strength to the case for modernisation. "Our Union is affiliated to the Labour Party— so let us be loyal to our own Government. Don't rock the boat, or we might get the Tories back. In any case, industrial action in pursuit of our demands will chase away customers and lose miners' jobs." Again, the "logic" is fearfully impressive.

On the other hand, if we do not compel the Government to change its policy, jobs will still be lost at a very rapid rate; and if we continue to accept the Coal Board's rejection of even the most moderate demands (for example, the 40-hour week for surface workers) we become ineffective and discredited as a Union and make progress, if at all, at a snail's pace.

There are those who believe we must accept the present rate of contraction and get the best bargain we can on the basis of improved productivity. There are those who believe we should demand a slow down in the rate of contraction to phase in with new industries and campaign on purely conventional lines for these objectives.

Is it possible—or advisable—to go further?

Would industrial action—*which can take more than one form*— really play into the hands of our enemies?

We are told by the Board that improvements cannot be conceded because increased costs will simply increase the coal stocks and close pits. But because these stocks are there, runs the argument, industrial action cannot be contemplated. We would emerge in a weaker bargaining position than ever before.

The argument is a vicious circle—and the miners will never escape from it unless they are bold enough to break out. And they will not break out unless they demonstrate to the Government and the Coal Board that this "logic" will not deter them in the pursuit of justice.

The economy of this country is still largely dependent on coal. Important sectors of the economy, including coal-fired power stations, are totally reliant on coal. A withdrawal of labour whether on a national scale or on a selective basis in each coalfield (with organised financial assistance by the Union for those involved) could make the Government realise that the miners' loyalty it not something to be coldly taken for granted.

And it would make the Coal Board realise that a rejection of justified demands in future would meet with an angry and effective response from the miners!

The most effective form of industrial action is something that should be seriously considered. Such action need not take the form of a prolonged national stoppage. Short sharp "guerilla" action has been used in other industries.

More so, if the possibility of such action was seriously contemplated, other Unions and their members could be approached for assistance. Workers employed on railways, road transport, and coastal shipping are experiencing a decline in jobs because of coal contraction. Those engaged in the manufacture of mining machinery and equipment are also affected. The possibilities of joint action with workers in these industries exist and should at least be explored.

Certainly there appears to be little chance of pursuing our claims with the desired measure of success unless we demonstrate our determination to take industrial action when other means have failed. Other trade unionists—from railwaymen and dockers to busmen and bank clerks—have shown some boldness in pursuit of their demands in recent years, and have achieved varying degrees of success. Meekness on our part will meet with no response. *By adopting more militant attitudes to secure a change in fuel policy we could save Britain from over-dependence on foreign fuel supplies. But we could also protect our mining communities from the worst effects of redundancy and win conditions and rewards that would attract and hold young, skilful and intelligent men in our modern coal industry.* The future of coal affects all our members and that is why they should be entitled to participate as fully as possible in the making of decisions that affect their lives. Through their trade union representatives on the Consultative Committees they should have access to all information, financial and otherwise, concerning the Board's operations. At colliery and every other level there should be maximum consultation with the Unions *before* decisions are taken. All too often consultation means deciding first and then in effect, telling the men to "take it or leave it". There is a strong case for a complete review of the industry's administration with a view to introducing a more democratic structure. This is not suggested as the ideal solution to all the problems of the industry. But, for a start, a thorough-going inquiry and some serious experimentation in forms of industrial democracy might produce some of the answers to the problems of industrial relations, about which there is so much talk and so little action.

There should be considered the possibility of reorganising, and renaming colliery consultative committees with effective powers on matters like hiring and firing, shift arrangements, team appointments and tasks and safety and health.

As pits are closed by the stroke of a pen at Hobart House, the consultative procedures become a grim and unpleasant farce conducive to the most cynical attitudes. Worse still when Lord Robens insists that the closing of these pits is being imposed upon them by a Labour Government. All of us want to see a Labour Government succeed and none of us, surely, would ever want to see the Tories back in power.

But as democrats we have not only the right but the duty to criticise our Labour Government if we sincerely believe that certain of its policies are mistaken. In criticising it we endeavour to be constructive and we make it clear that what we desire is *not a change of Government but a change of policy.*

As a member of the Labour Party I emphatically disagree with those who say that the answer might lie in the formation of a new trade Union Political party. And I disagree with those who advocate withdrawal of the political levy from the Labour Party. Such measures can only weaken and divide our movement and reduce the influence of the miners within our own Party.

The real alternative is to work for the implementation of radical policies by the Government designed to take Britain in the direction of a Socialist society.. This alternative was outlined by the Trades Union Congress last year when it demanded that the Government should make full us of all *indigenous* resources and should:—

1. Maintain full employment.
2. Effectively control both import and export of capital.
3. Increase its efforts with regard to world trade and development.
4. Drastically reduce military expenditure.

Institute for Workers' Control

PUBLICATIONS

Hugh Scanlon: *The Way Forward for Workers' Control*   1/6d
Michael Barratt Brown: *Opening the Books*   1/6d
Michael Barratt Brown: *Labour & Sterling*   1/6d
Tony Topham: *Productivity Bargaining & Workers' Control*   1/6d
Ken Coates & Tony Topham: *Participation or Control?*   1/6d
Ken Coates & Tony Topham: *Labour's Plan for Industrial Democracy*   1/6d
Bob Harrison & Walter Kendall: *Workers' Control and the Motor Industry*   1/6d
No Bus Today   1/6d
The Dockers' Next Step   1/6d
Report of the 1967 Workers' Control Conference   10/-
A Future for British Socialism? Record of the Scarborough teach in on Workers' Control   5/-

DUPLICATED TRACTS

Ray Collins: *Workers' Control in Wales*   1/-
Antonio Gramsci: *Two Articles on Workers' Control & Revolution*   1/-
Nick Hillier: *Farmworkers' Control*   1/-

ARCHIVES IN TRADE UNION HISTORY AND THEORY

A very limited number of sets at £1

Titles including:

De Brouckere: *How to Win Workers' Control*
Ablett and others: *The Miners' Next Step.*
Allen: *Revolutionary Unionism.*
The Daily Herald: *Report on the Leeds Convention, 1917.*
Hodges & Sankey, and the MFGB: *Mines Nationalisation.*
South Wales Socialist Society: *Industrial Democracy For Miners.*
Tom Mann: *Prepare For Action, Forging The Weapon.*
Labour Party—TUC statement: *The Waste of Capitalism.*
Extracts From Union Rules.

BOOKS

Industrial Democracy in Great Britain, by Ken Coates & Tony Topham   63/-
Can the Workers Run Industry? Edited by Ken Coates   9/6d

INSTITUTE FOR WORKERS' CONTROL

A Socialist Strategy for Western Europe

ERNEST MANDEL

Pamphlet No. 10 Third Impression   Price 10p

Ernest Mandel

A SOCIALIST STRATEGY FOR WESTERN EUROPE

The debate over socialist strategy in western Europe must start from the prior assumption that, during the next decade, there will be neither a world nuclear war nor an economic crisis of comparable gravity with that of 1929-1933. It is not hard to see why we must limit our discussion by making this assumption: either one of the two alternatives would mean that the problem was completely transformed, in both its objective and subjective aspects. Nor need we waste much time on the reasons why it is plausible to make such an assumption. If the United States ruling class chose to unleash a world nuclear war in any *concrete* situation, except one in which it was directly threatened with extinction, it would simply be committing suicide. Even if the possibility cannot be entirely ruled out—and there is also the possibility of a war unleashed through error or insanity—it is not one on which we could (or need) build a strategy for the workers' movement.

As far as an economic crisis or catastrophe is concerned, it has been emphasized and re-emphasized that there are strong reasons why this can be avoided by neo-capitalism for a considerable tome to come.[1] To go over the principle points very briefly: the size of the State budget and State intervention in the economy; the use of a whole arsenal of anti crisis techniques; the use of "public investment" (particularly armaments) to compensate for any sagging in private investment, etc.

[1] Ernest Mandel, *L'Apogée du néo-capitalisme et ses lendemains* in *Les Temps Modernes*, August-September, 1964.

Certainly, the capitalist regime cannot transform threatening crises into mild recessions completely unscathed. There is a twofold price to pay for the conversion: first, a lasting tendency towards inflation and a loss of purchasing power of leading currencies; second, an increasingly widespread surplus productive capacity (the other face of the coin of over-production). Without doubt, these two factors will make themselves strongly felt during the coming decade; already the United States payments deficit, and the ensuing dollar crisis, are giving the neo-capitalist success story a sharp jolt. But there is no reason to doubt that the system will be able to go on functioning, though rather bumpily, through several more monetary crises and anyway for a decade.

Finally, it should be said that, during the next decade, the colonial revolution will probably make further advances and we can also expect spectacular developments in the socialist countries; however, neither of these will *basically* alter the economic and social situation of the imperialist world (though of course they will have an undeniable influence, which there is no need to go into here).

It should also be remembered that those taking part in this discussion do not believe that social reforms of the type associated with the Swedish social-democratic government or the post-war Labour government in Britain can change the capitalist character of the economy or society in any way or serve as models for a socialist strategy whose purpose is the overthrow of capitalism.

Discussion must take place within this limited context; the various proposals on socialist strategy in western Europe cannot be evaluated outside this framework.

It does not follow that because there are no catastrophic economic crises there are no crises at all.

The first problem for marxists to face is the following: since we have established, as our initial hypothesis, that we cannot expect any catastrophic economic crisis comparable with 1929-1932 (or any near collapse of the bourgeois state, as occurred after defeat in war: Germany 1918-19, Italy 1943-45, etc.), does this imply that there will be no crisis at all to threaten the capitalist economy, society and State?

This is a crucial question, because only idealists—in the philosophical-sociological sense—can envisage the overthrow of capitalism without any kind of social, political or economic crisis. In such a case, the overthrow of capitalism would follow simply on a *prise de conscience* by the great majority of the working population (or else a putsch!) To accept a hypothesis of this kind would mean backsliding into utopianism.

For a marxist, there is no doubt that we can only approach the problems of the overthrow of capitalism and the conquest of power by starting with the objective conditions in which the masses could be mobilized and the situations of breakdown in which the balance of social forces within bourgeois society is upset. These are what we call " crisis situations ". But these situations are not necessarily the same as crises of catastrophic over-production, except for mechanistic determinist economists, who are far from being marxists.

First of all, it should be emphasized that, though we consider that neo-capitalism is perfectly capable of converting serious over-production crises into milder and briefer recessions, we do not think it capable of suppressing its repeated short-term fluctuations. The American economy experienced regular recessions, in 1949, 1953, 1957-58, 1960-61. And I have tried to explain elsewhere the reasons for the *temporary* shortening of the cycle, and the reasons which suggest that there can be no *conclusive* shortening of it.

The American economy is the typical economy of the neo-capitalist system in the imperialist countries: it is the model which western Europe and Japan imitate with a lag of several years. It therefore seems very likely that when these countries emerge from the special cycle of the re-construction period, their economies will experience the same kind of recessions, although this has not happened as yet (I am talking of countries such as Great Britain, Belgium and, recently, Italy and France).

These economic fluctuations will then themselves produce the mechanisms which *can* periodically disturb the balance of the capitalist societies and States; the difference between these milder recessions and more serious crises mainly being that the socio-political consequences are *much less automatic* (after the 1929-33 crisis there were serious political and social repercussions in every capitalist country).

The explosive factors in present-day society are not restricted to those coming from these short-term economic fluctuations. There are also a number of unanswered structural problems: the problem of the *Mezzogiorno* in Italy and the general problem of under-developed or declining regions; the problem of German unification; the problem of the downfall or extinction of the semi-fascist regimes of Spain and Portugal and the repercussions which would follow their revolutionary overthrow; attempts to establish " strong government " in other European countries; the constant possibility of monetary and financial crises, which on occasion can have very sharp effects (cf. the consequences of the banking crisis which has recently occurred in Uruguay, " the Switzerland of Latin America "); the constant possibility that any major social conflict will take a political form and provoke retaliation by the State (with the possible ensuing counter-retaliation of the working class movement and the working masses).

To put it in more general terms: we need not believe, simply because the neo-capitalist system has succeeded in avoiding catastrophic economic crises, that it is therefore capable of *solving all the economic and social problems* which face it. We do not believe that this system has, in the slightest way, resolved the basic contradictions of the capitalist mode of production. And we believe that, to these classical contradictions, it adds a whole series of new contradictions of its own.

In analyzing neo-capitalism, people often make the mistake of thinking that " solutions " which in fact create sharp new contradictions are evidence of a " conflict-less situation ". I have already given one example,[3] which springs from one of neo-capitalism's apparently spectacular successes: long-term high employment. This " solution " inevitably leads to constant wage-rises, which finally end up by threatening to cut the rate of profit in a decisive way. Hence the necessity for the bourgeoisie of limiting or abolishing trade union independence in negotiating wages (incomes policies, etc.). Hence also the tendency to replace extensive by intensive investments, substituting depth for breadth, in order to economize on man-power (automation). All these developments tend to bring the crisis in the trade union movement to a head, rather than integrating it further into the State and eliminating conflict.

The problem of incomes policy gives rise to a larger problem which, in fact, has grown more serious under neo-capitalism than under classical capitalism: how can there be a constant and harmonious rise in the purchasing power of the wage-earners in a capitalist regime? To the extent that the capitalist system requires a multiplicity of decision centres, regarding both prices and investments,[4] it will be unable to avoid periodic fluctuations

---

[3] Ibid.
[4] " Capital only exists and can only exist in the form of numerous separate capitals and, for this reason, its self-determination will be manifested as the mutual inter-action of these capitals ". (Karl Marx: *Grundrisse der Kritik der Politischen Oekonomie*, p. 317, Dietz-Verlag, Berlin, 1953.

in real wages, out of step with the periodic fluctuations of the real cost of living. And, as the system becomes more and more a prey to international competition, there will also be periodic lags in the levels of real wages in different imperialist countries, which means that management will have to launch periodic attacks on " excessive wage rises ". And as long as there is an independent working class movement (and, above all, an independent trade union movement) these periodic attacks by management will create at least objectively favourable conditions for the explosion of more far-reaching social struggle, which challenge the whole operation of the capitalist economy and might even lead to victorious workers' counter-attacks.

Similarly, if neo-capitalism cannot survive without periodic management attacks on " excessive " wage rises, it will not be able to avoid attacking the level of employment; it might even be said, under neo-capitalism, that recessions are more or less deliberately *provoked* by the bourgeoisie—principally as a result of deflationist squeezes—as well as occurring through the internal mechanisms of capitalism. Thus we have another example of objectively favourable conditions for an extensive struggle, particularly *at the turning-point when the recession sets in,* which has always been the most preferable time for working class struggles under classical capitalism.

Affluence does not mean that the workers feel there is nothing left to fight for.

If we accept that, although there will be no catastrophic crisis of the 1929-33 type, this does not mean that there will be no economic and social contradictions which could arouse far-reaching workers' struggles, then it follows that the vanguard forces within the workers' movement must put forward a whole series of objectives to galvanize the masses. The examples given above—struggle against rises in the cost of living, against various kinds of wage-freeze or " controlled growth of incomes ", against recurrent waves of lay-offs—must be prominent features of the appropriate campaign.

These are essentially *defensive* objectives. But neo-capitalism is bringing with it, nationally and internationally, a new phase in the development of the productive forces. There must be a new roster of workers' objectives, corresponding to the development of these forces and qualitatively and quantitatively different from those of the past.

Wages are the price of labour power; the price of labour power oscillates around its value. Now, Marx stresses that this value is not a stable physiological datum but a datum made up of variable historical and geographical factors. And he insists on the fact that new needs can and should be incorporated from time to time into the variable element of wages, which is evidence of the civilizing quality of trade union action.[5]

As the undeniable rise in the standard of living and real wages of the working class has reduced the proportion of purchasing power expended on basic nourishment and everyday clothing, the working class in the imperialist countries has developed a whole series of new needs which play an increasingly important role in its daily preoccupations: housing, transport, children's education, holidays, safety and, especially, protection against disease and unemployment. Corresponding to all these needs—whose satisfaction is under-developed or warped under capitalism—there are new forms of social consumption and socialization of the costs of satisfaction, which suggest a quite different model of distribution of the national income.

The more affluent he becomes, the more the worker runs up against new forms of alienation, supplementing the old. He is not alienated only as a producer; he is also alienated as a consumer. Any number of examples could be given of the way in which the so-called " successes " of neo-capitalism create new problems: the deterioration in quality of a whole series of mass consumption goods; the traumatic effects of increasingly intrusive advertizing; the danger that new forms of leisure (such as TV!) will lead to class atomization. The working class movement can and must apply new solutions to these new problems—solutions which challenge the capitalist mode of production as such.

But, although workers are undergoing increased alienation as consumers, they are nonetheless alienated, first and foremost, as producers. During the neo-capitalist period, this alienation is given new dimensions arising from the very mechanisms which, for the time being, bring neo-capitalism its successes: the permanent technological revolution, the third industrial revolution, ever-spreading automation. The problems involved—control over speed-up and lay-offs; control over the organization of production; the effective role of the producer in the system—descend from the heady realms of philosophy to take their place, poten-

---

[5] Rosa Luxemburg, " The chief function of trade unions is that, by adding to the needs of the workers and raising them morally, it creates a cultural and social vital minimum in the stead of a physical vital minimum—in other words, it creates a definite level of cultural life for the workers ". (*Einführung in die Nationalökonomie*, p. 275, E. Laubsche Verlagsbuchhandlung, Berlin, 1925).

tially at least, in the day-to-day trade union struggle. Everything connected with this group of problems is becoming increasingly important to the workers: the opportunity follows of raising the struggle for union demands onto a new level. If I may quote my own work: " In the same way that the daily experience of the nineteenth century worker taught him how the net product of each enterprise was divided between wages and profits, the daily experience of the worker in the neo-capitalist period teaches him how the national income is divided between the total of earned and the total of unearned income and how these mechanisms can only be mastered by the seizure of the means of production, the " levers of power " of the whole of economic life." [6]

All the objectives I have listed above are *potentially revolutionary*, in the sense that they challenge the capitalist nature of the economy and the nature of the private ownership of the means of production themselves. And they are not merely ideological issues, but immediate aims of the masses. So, far from postponing the socialist revolution till the very distant future, neo-capitalism actually brings to fruition a series of circumstances which present revolution as an immediate and urgent necessity, demanded *by the facts*, without having to wait for the workers to understand the Theses on Feuerbach or the Third Volume of Capital first.

The Strategy of Structural Reforms.

The main purpose of the strategy of structural reforms—invented by the left wing of the Belgian working class movement and now increasingly adopted by its counterparts throughout Europe—is to effect an integration between the immediate aims of the masses and the objectives of the struggle which objectively challenge the very existence of the capitalist system itself.

It does not mean in the slightest that the workers' movement abandons wage claims, demands for shorter hours, the insistence on a sliding scale to combat the rising cost of living, etc.—all the traditional demands of the movement (or at least of its left wing). But it does mean that the movement does not *limit* itself to these immediate objectives or to a combination of struggle for these objectives together with vague propaganda for the " socialist revolution ", the " socialization of the means of production ", even " the dictatorship of the proletariat ", which, while they are not part and parcel of the daily struggle,

[6] *Traité d'Economie Marxist*., II, p. 198.

can exert no influence on the practical development of the class struggle.[7] It means that the working class movement, *in its day-by-day struggle,* combines the fight for immediate objectives which, rooted in the immediate interests of the masses, go on to challenge objectively the operation of the capitalist system.

There is no doubt that this is a daring strategy; it carries grave risks. The main risk is that we live in a period of development of the productive forces, in which the representatives of the most dynamic and aggressive sectors of capitalism themselves have an interest in various structural transformations of the economy. If the workers' movement is not vigilant, *it therefore risks lending its support to neo-capitalist strata,* who are engaged in a struggle against more conservative capitalist forces, whose interests are best served by the existing structures.

In other word, the formula of " structural reforms " can be interpreted in two diametrically opposite ways: either it can mean *a reform of capitalism whose purpose is to ensure that the economy will function more satisfactorily* or it can mean " reforms " extorted by the working class struggle, completely incompatible with the normal operation of any kind of capitalist economy. These latter inaugurate a period in which there is a duality of power, whose conclusion must be either a defeat for the working class (in which case the " reforms " are destroyed) or a defeat for the bourgeoisie (in which case the " reforms " are consolidated by the conquest of power by the proletariat and the socialization of the means of production, democratically managed by the workers themselves).

In the first case, we are dealing with " *neo-capitalist structural reforms* ", the principal trap into which the socialist left in western Europe could fall; in the second case we are dealing with " *anti-capitalist structural reforms* ", which are the main way forward for a socialist strategy in Europe.

Since the term " structural reform " is naturally ambiguous, it is not good enough to try and distinguish an aggressive socialist strategy from a reformist social-democratic policy (essentially

---

[7] We should not forget that the classic reformists of the beginning of the century did not in the slightest turn their backs on socialist propaganda. Reformism only abandons this propaganda in the final phase of its degeneration and then starts to jettison all references to socialist ideals or actually recants from them. So the real difference between socialist and reformist *action* cannot be seen in terms of whether there is socialist propaganda or not. The essential question is that of objectives for practical struggles: either these are limited to what can be achieved within a capitalist regime and digested by it or else they challenge the very existence of the regime, both by their goals and by their size.

a support or even temporary consolidation of neo-capitalism) simply by applying different labels or even by making more comprehensive definitions. But, without claiming to have said everything there is to say, I would like to put forward five characteristics of a strategy of anti-capitalist structural reforms, which go together and which are indispensable if the neo-capitalist trap is to be avoided:

1. We must not try to capture " outlying positions " from capitalism as a first step, under the illusion that we will thereby lessen resistance and be able to advance " step by step " towards the heart of the capitalist fortress. Experience persistently teaches us that the nationalization of non-central sectors, or of raw material and energy producing sectors, if it is carried out apart from a general forward movement on all fronts, can be integrated without any trouble into the general scheme of rationalizing (and hence consolidating) the capitalist economy.

Moreover, it is utterly impossible to operate an economy " at the same time " according to the criteria of collective interests and the criteria of the private interests of the big capitalists. There cannot be any consonance between these two criteria, when basic economic choices are at stake. Either the criterion of profit is uppermost, in which case the operation of the whole economy must necessarily be *subordinated* to the demands and profitability of the major monopolistic groups (which is perfectly compatible with the nationalization of specific sectors, socializing losses and providing state subsidies or hidden savings for the monopolies) or else things are taken to a different conclusion and private property must be abolished, if the whole economy is not to grind to a halt.

So the attack must be made, not on outlying sectors, *but on the key sectors,* the sectors which provide the bulk of the national income and the greatest volume and dynamic of investment, the " commanding heights " of the economy. Unless we try to seize these key sectors from capitalism, our policies will be not anti-capitalist but neo-capitalist, whatever our intentions may be.

2. We must raise the question of the hierarchic structure of the enterprise, of the power of decision over the organization of work, of workers' control over production (which can as easily spring from micro-economic problems, at enterprise level, as from such macro-economic problems as profit levels, price and credit policies, causes of inflation, etc.), the abolition of commercial and banking secre s and the opening of the books.

This is the only way to avoid giving the strategy of structural reforms a technocratic character and giving it life in the factories, on the shopfloor and in offices, of tieing in closely to the mass of workers themselves. It is also the only way of making the duality of power a real threat to the survival of capitalism.

3. We must resolutely reject the institutionalization of workers' control and the institutionalization of anti-capitalist structural reforms in general. First and foremost, because otherwise we would be being utopian; it cannot be emphasized enough that no economy can function in practice according to two criteria, two sets of demands, two models of consumption, two opposed and contradictory powers in each enterprise. Secondly, because this is a trap, a very dangerous trap, which recalls the most vulgar reformist illusions: Léon Jouhaux imagined that he had already " started " to change the nature of capitalism the day he was named governor of the Bank of France! An army cannot be taken apart " battalion by battalion " any more than capitalism can be abolished " step by step ". In practice, the institutionalization of workers' control in a context in which big capitalism would still control the main wealth and power points of the economy as a whole would quickly deprive it of any real substance and would turn it into a means of corrupting working class militants.

4. The programme of anti-capitalist structural reforms must be closely connected with a clear governmental formula, defining the replacement in power of one class by another (in Belgium, we use the formula: a workers' government based on the unions).[8] This is of the utmost importance, for it is essential to bring home to mass of the workers that the question of structural reforms leads on to *the question of power* and that it is the struggle for power which will finally decide the issue of the battle. There is no need here to point out how illusions about putting through structural reforms " stage by stage " find their reflection in illusions about coalitions with the bourgeoisie which could put through this programme " bit by bit ".

[8] This is an algebraic formula, unaffected by the form of organization adopted by christian workers (a key question, in both Belgium in Italy) or by the establishment of an independent christian workers party, or by their entry *en bloc* into a socialist organization or by their alliance with other working class parties.

5. Propaganda for anti-capitalist structural reforms must be accompanied by an intense and systematic critique of capitalism as a whole, of its contradictions and its ludicrous methods of production, of its more and more idiotic and alienating model of consumption, of the monstrous social inequality which it continues to sustain—in short, by a systematic socialist education, which opposes the idea of socialist planning to the idea of capitalist "programming". This propaganda must also *play its part in demystifying,* in revealing the reality hidden behind ‘phrases like " improving the workings of the economy " (read: the capitalist economy), " stabilizing the purchasing power of money ", ensuring " a steady rate of growth ", and so on and so forth.

The working masses are ready and waiting for a strategy of this kind.

The relatively high standard of living which the workers enjoy during the neo-capitalist period (until the long-term cycle marked by economic growth reaches its end and the financial crisis caused by incessant inflation brings about new explosions) is often said to make a strategy of anti-capitalist structural reforms, such as I have outlined, a utopian prospect. It is argued that, since it is no longer impelled to action by hunger, misery and massive unemployment, the working mass is destined for " americanization ", that is to say, de-politicization, the loss of its class consciousness under the influence of the mass media, which feed it ever more homogenous and co-ordinated propaganda, or, at the very least, for a persistent process of fragmentation, both at and away from work, as a result of automation.[9]

This is an important objection, which must be fully dealt with. I have shown above how neo-capitalism does not in fact put an end to the causes of workers' discontent and that it is still quite possible to launch powerful campaigns—perhaps even inevitable. But can these campaigns take on a revolutionary complexion, in the context of a welfare society? Or are they necessarily restricted to reformist objectives, as long as they

---

[9] There is obviously a great difference between the situation in the United States where, for well-known historical reasons, the proletariat has never attained political class consciousness—so that the class struggle is only a trade union struggle—and western Europe, where working class political apathy means that there has been a *loss* of class consciousness built up over half a century. It is quite likely that the American proletariat will end up by being politicized before the depoliticization of the European working class has become complete.

take place in an atmosphere of more or less general prosperity? In other words, can "americanized" or "depoliticized" workers respond to anything else than reformism, even when they are fighting a wage-freeze, murderous speed-up or snowballing technological unemployment?

Before replying to this objection, we must first look at it more closely. If the objection is referring to the fact that, in the present economic atmosphere, there are going to be no repetitions of the 1918 German revolution or the 1941-45 Yugoslav revolution, then it is no more than a truism. We have already admitted this truism and included it in our prior hypothesis. And that brings us to the real point: are these particular kinds of revolution the only ones which can achieve the overthrow of capitalism? Are "catastrophic" conditions necessary? No. There is a different historic model which we can refer to: that of the general strike of June 1936 in France (and, to a lesser extent, the Belgian general strike of 1960-61, which came near to creating an analogous situation to that of 1936).

It is perfectly possible that, in the present general economic climate—that of "neo-capitalist affluence" or the "mass consumption society",—the workers will become more and more radicalized as the result of a whole series of social, political, economic or even military crises (incomes policies, wage-freezes; anti-union measures, authoritarianism; recessions, sudden monetary crises; protest movements against imperialist aggression, imperialist military alliances, the use of tactical nuclear weapons in so-called wars, etc.) and that, once they are radicalized, they will launch more and more far-reaching campaigns, during the course of which they will begin to link their immediate demands with a programme of anti-capitalist structural reforms, until eventually the struggle concludes with a general strike which either overthrows the regime or creates a duality of powers.[10]

Naturally, all this pre-supposes a growing *prise de conscience* rather than a relapse into political apathy. But there is nothing unrealistic or utopian about this hypothesis. The experience of the last five years has shown how there is no automatic correlation between high wage rates (comparatively high on an international scale) and political apathy. In Italy, an unprecedented climb in wage rates has led to the strengthening of the Communist Party at the polls. In Belgium, the 1960-61 strike

---

[10] It would require a separate study to deal with the particular problems raised by the duality of powers.

was called at a time when Belgian wage rates were among the highest in Europe, and its staunchest adherents were the best-paid sector of the Belgian working-class: the Liège iron and steel workers. And it could hardly be claimed that it was any fall in wages which led the working masses of Britain to elect the 1964 Labour gouvernment and oust the crestfallen tories.

Furthermore, the present situation of the western European workers' movement is extremely variegated; there are a multitude of nuances between its two extremes; on the one hand, there is the workers' movement in West Germany; the Netherlands or Switzerland, where autonomous class action and a comparatively high level of consciousness are only to be found among small, isolated groups (which does not necessarily mean that this will be the case for ever); on the other hand, there is Italy, Great Britain or Belgium, where, for all its weaknesses (and I am only too well aware of those in Belgium!), the workers' movement still displays a high level of autonomous class action, with a rich and diverse ideological life, a remarkable and widespread degree of combativity and genuine opportunities for making a real breakthrough.

Now, it is not possible to explain the differences between these two different sets of examples, simply by referring to their different objective conditions. Average wage rates in Britain are still among the highest in western Europe; the same is true of Belgium (and since Belgian rates have relatively begun to fall back, the aggressive dynamism of the workers' movement has also fallen back with them, rather than surged forward); Italian wage rates have been rising faster than any others in Europe, for many years. It is quite untenable to explain the enormous differences in dynamism between the movements in Belgium and the Netherlands by referring to the objective conditions (and, in any case, Dutch wage rates have been comparatively low for two decades); the same is true of the differences between the French and Italian movements, over the last five years. It is quite clear that we are dealing with a whole complex of factors, among which that of " relative prosperity " cannot be shown to be particularly dominant.

It follows that *it is above all the subjective factor which plays the key role* in deciding whether or not the workers' movement makes use of the *opportunity* which neo-capitalism provides for an anti-capitalist strategic offensive. That is to say, in the last analysis everything depends on the action of the working class movement itself.

Here we can put our finger on the objective conditions which confront us today and those of, say, the thirties. During a period in which the worker is not irresistibly impelled against capitalism by hunger or misery, anti-capitalist action ceases to be the *automatic* result of his daily experience. But it can become so *through the mediation, the awakening of consciousness, which is the task of the workers' movement*. If the workers' movement is capable of fulfilling its task (not only little vanguard groups, but also those trade union and political forces which influence parts of the working class) it can throw a bridge, by action and education, between essentially defensive struggles (which are inevitable, though not " automatic ") and struggles which can conclude objectively in the overthrow of the capitalist system. If on the contrary, it falls short, then undeniably there will be a process of gradual degradation and deterioration of class consciousness, of working class depoliticization, until the West German or Swiss model is arrived at, in which, as far as can be seen, the great majority of the working class no longer wants any part in far-reaching anti-capitalist struggles.

International co-ordination of the struggle.

There are two further problems which remain to be discussed: the problem of periodicity and the problem of the implications of European economic integration.

Any socialist strategy which is *based on mass action* (rather than electoral campaigns or guerrilla wars) must necessarily pay great attention to fluctuations in mass psychology, state of mind and relative capacity to respond to blows from the enemy and move on to the attack. Obviously, this capacity is not static. No individual—and *a fortiori* no group of individuals—can live over a long period, uninterruptedly, in a state of extreme tension. Theoretically and empirically, it has long since been shown that there are periodic fluctuations in the degree of mass action, no matter which country is being considered.

There is no need, in this context, to describe the delicate mechanism of inter-action between objective and subjective factors which explains this periodicity. Evidently, this is *related* to the economic cycle; but this relationship certainly does not mean that the peak point of mass action occurs when economic activity is in a trough. I have already pointed out that this peak point is much more likely to occur *at the time when the economic trend is reversed* (first waves of lay-offs or the favourable effect of full employment on the balance of class power).

The problem is complicated, however, because there is both a short-term and a long-term cycle of mass action (for example, in France the defeat of the workers' movement by the arrival in power of De Gaulle has led to conditions completely different from those prevalent in Italy). Various historical factors—the level of class consciousness attained in the past; the continuing influence of past forms of struggle—also have a considerable effect on the periodicity of struggles. The cycle can be slowed down or speeded up according to whether there is a greater or lesser degree of class unity. And there are many other important factors which might be listed.

It is of the utmost importance that *the internal logic of the periodicity of the workers' struggles* should be geared to the strategy outlined above. Obviously, a growing intensity of radicalization, enabling the struggle to be set more and more towards anti-capitalist objectives, must co-incide with a growing intensity of *mass* action in the cycle or else it will be doomed to failure, after which it may take as much as a decade or more to recover. It is also obvious that if we *let slip* the peak moments of mass struggle, without linking them to struggles for anti-capitalist reforms, we shall lose the chance of launching a decisive campaign for many years to come. In the present atmosphere, we cannot expect the proletariat, in western Europe at least, to launch a general strike every two years. A number of factors are of crucial importance: a correct analysis of the state of mind of the masses; the balance of power between the vanguard and the more retrograde and conservative forces within the workers' movement; the ability to produce the right slogans at the right moment, and so on and so forth. All these factors are crucial if a socialist strategy is to be applied with the least hope of success.

Concerning the European co-ordination of the struggle, I have already written at length elsewhere.[11] For as long as the working class in each of the six Common Market countries is able to exert pressure on the productive system of " its " country and " its " bourgeoisie, the best solution would be a country-by-country struggle, so that a victory in one would lead to favourable conditions for an international campaign against the movement towards the Common Market, NATO and other international organizations, sabotaging or destroying their effectiveness.

On the other hand, from the time that the interpenetration of capital reaches a certain point, there will be less and less possibility of an isolated victory in a single Common Market country and there will be a very strong likelihood that any

---

[11] Cf. my report to the seminar on *Intégration européenne et mouvement ouvrier*, organized by *Cahiers du Centre d'Etudes socialistes* in Paris.

isolated socialist experiment could be economically and financially strangulated. From this point on, the possibility of a socialist breakthrough must be an all or nothing affair, involving the whole Common Market. It must be admitted that this means a turn for the worse, at least in the short and middle term (in the long term, it has definite advantages). For whereas the first alternative requires a high degree of mass action and a successful outcome in only one country, the second requires a high degree of mass action in each country simultaneously, *co-inciding* with a successful simultaneous outcome! Obviously this is the harder to come by.

Spokesman Books is the publishing imprint of the Bertrand Russell Peace Foundation Ltd. We publish in many areas including politics, peace and disarmament, history, drama and philosophy. Visit our website for more information:

www.spokesmanbooks.org

The Institute for Workers' Control was formed in 1968, building on a series of conferences over several years to encourage discussion and communication between shop stewards, workers' control groups and trade unions, and to publish important materials on industrial democracy and workers' control throughout the world.

Socialist Renewal grew out of the discussion around Labour's abandonment of its Clause Four commitment to public ownership in 1995. A general invitation was issued to socialist authors to write for the series. Many pamphlets and books followed. Some texts and details of all publications can be found on the Socialist Renewal website:

www.socialistrenewal.net